BOOK OF JOHN

100 Days of Discipleship
Verse by verse question/answer Study

Angie Meadows

Angie Meadows

Study based on the NKJV Bible version.

A Thousand Tears, LLC
PO Box 1373
Huntington, WV 25715

© 2011, 2024 Angie G Meadows

All rights reserved. No portion of this publication may be reproduced, stored in a retrieval system, or transmitted in any form or by any means—electronic, mechanical, photocopy, recording, or any other—without the prior written permission of the author.

> *I love them that love me,*
> *and those that seek me*
> *diligently will find me.*
>
> *Proverbs 8:17*

Study Hints: When you begin this study, pray God will enlighten your eyes to see and open your ears to hear truth. The main themes of John are: Come, Follow, Believe, Abide and Life. Write down the main word(s) or theme from every verse and then go back through at the end of each chapter and pray for the ability to obey the truths that you have learned. This is a journey of growing that enables us to believe as we learn to die to our own will and go to the grave of self and arise with newness of life with His glorious resurrection power and learn to faithfully abide in Christ. Blessings for *your* journey.

Table of Contents

Book of John 1

John 1 5

John 2 29

John 3 39

John 4 56

John 5 76

John 6 97

John 7 127

John 8 148

John 9 176

John 10 196

John 11 217

John 12 239

John 13 259

John 14 275

John 15 291

John 16 304

John 17 322

John 18 337

John 19 360

John 20 381

John 21 395

   Appendix A 406

The Morning Watch: The Sweet Fragrance of God. 406

John 1

Jesus is the Word

In the beginning was the Word, and the Word was with God, and the Word was God. John 1:1

Day 1

1. A. Who was in the beginning?

   B. Who was with God?

   C. Who was the Word?

John 1:1 NKJV
In the beginning was the Word, and the Word was with God, and the Word was God.

2. From the beginning was Jesus, the Word. Was Jesus always with God?

John 1:2 NKJV
He was in the beginning with God.

3. All things were made by whom?

John 1:3 NKJV

All things were made through Him, and without Him nothing was made that was made.

4. A. Who is life?

   B. Who is the light of men?

John 1:4 NKJV
In Him was life, and the life was the light of men.

5. A. Who shines in darkness?

   B. What does the darkness represent?

John 1:5 NKJV
And the light shines in the darkness, and the darkness did not comprehend it.

Answers:
1. A. The Word was in the beginning. B. The Word (John 1:14) was with God. C. The Word was God.
2. Yes, Jesus was always with God.
3. All things were made by Jesus Christ/the Word.
4. A. Life is Jesus Christ. B. Jesus is the light illuminating the darkness.
5. A. Jesus is the light that shines in the darkness. B. Darkness represents evil, or maybe spiritual blindness.

Outline:
- Jesus is God and the Word. They are all one. We will develop this theme of oneness within the trinity throughout the book of John.
- Jesus is eternal as God is eternal.
- When God created the earth in Genesis, he spoke, and his Words had creative power. The Word of God creates. Without the Word in our lives our creativeness will be squelched.
- Without Jesus I can't see. I will be stumbling in the darkness. This will be evident by confusion in my life. Jesus is the light of the world.

Thoughts to ponder:
1. Was Jesus from the beginning in Genesis?

2. Is faith intellectual or is it a journey of revelation through the guidance of the Holy Spirit?

3. If my life has confusion, can I stand still in the darkness and pray for the light to come?

Challenge: Look up the word "light". Write out a couple of verses that you would like to ponder.

How can you be a light to others in a dark world?

How can you practice healthy self-talk and become a light for yourself?

Write a prayer and ask for the guidance of the Holy Spirit. Surrender any areas of confusion.

Book of John

Day 2

Jesus is the True Light

But as many as received him, to them he gave power to become the sons of God... John 1:12

1. Who was this, John? Was he John the Baptist (the forerunner to Jesus Christ) or John the disciple (the author of the book of John)?

John 1:6 NKJV
There was a man sent from God, whose name was John.

2. What was John the Baptist's two purposes?

John 1:7 NKJV
This man came for a witness, to bear witness of the Light, that all through him might believe.

3. Was John the Baptist the light?

John 1:8 NKJV
He was not that Light but was sent to bear witness of that Light.

4. A. Who was the true light?

   B. Who was the light for?

John 1:9 NKJV

That was the true Light which gives light to every man coming into the world.

5.   A. Who was in the world?

      B. Who made the world?

      C. Did the world know Jesus?

John 1:10 NKJV
He was in the world, and the world was made through Him, and the world did not know Him.

6.   A. Who was His own?

      B. Did they receive Him?

John 1:11 NKJV
He came to His own, and His own did not receive Him.

7.   A. If a person believed in Jesus, what did he receive?

      B. What was the evidence that a person had received Jesus?

John 1:12 NKJV
But as many as received Him, to them He gave the right to become children of God, to those who believe in His name:

8.   Born means what? * This is a spiritual birth.

* The will of God is that no man should perish.

Book of John

John 1:13 NKJV
who were born, not of blood, nor of the will of the flesh, nor of the will of man, but of God.

9. A. Who was made flesh?

   B. Where did He dwell?

   C. What did Jesus have and why?

   D. What filled Jesus?

John 1:14 NKJV
And the Word became flesh and dwelt among us, and we beheld His glory, the glory as of the only begotten of the Father, full of grace and truth.

10. Who did John bare witness of?

*John declared Jesus was before him in existence.
John 1:15 NKJV
John bore witness of Him and cried out, saying, "This was He of whom I said, 'He who comes after me is preferred before me, for He was before me.'"

Answers:
1. John the Baptist the prophesied forerunner to the Messiah.
2. He was to be a witness to the Light. This witness of the light for all people that they might believe.
3. No, John was sent to bear witness of the light.
4. A. Jesus Christ is the true light. B. This light was for every man (human).
5. A. Jesus Christ came to this world. B. Jesus Christ made this world. C. But the world did not recognize Jesus.
6. A. The Jews were his people. B. No, the Jews did not receive Him.
7. A. Belief gives us the power to become the son of God. B. Evidence of belief is that a person believes on His name.
8. A spiritual birth is by the will of God.
9. A. God was made flesh in Jesus Christ. B. Jesus dwelled among us. C. Jesus beheld the glory of God because he was the only begotten Son of the Father. D. Jesus was filled with grace and truth.
10. John bore witness of Jesus.

Outline:
- Belief is the theme.
- Belief gives us power to become children of God.
- Jesus has always been and always will be.
- John the Baptist Matthew 11:14 is the prophesied Elijah to come. Malachi 4:5-6.

Things to Ponder:
1. Could receiving each other in fellowship meet an emotionally need to be known, seen, and validated by others?

2. Are you emotionally a safe space for other people?

3. Could you receive more of God's glory by giving yourself and others more grace and truth?

Challenge: Look up the phrase children of God and write a verse that the Holy Spirit highlights.

Did your parents give you a healthy view of God?

If not, you may struggle with authority. Ask God to help you see Him as a loving, protective Father.

Write a prayer and ask God to give you a belief that leads to the power to become a child of God.

Angie Meadows

Day 3

A call for a heart change.

He said, I am the voice of one crying in the wilderness, make straight the way of the Lord... John 1:23

1. A. What have we received?

   B. What is Jesus's fullness in the New Testament?

John 1:16 NKJV
And of His fullness we have all received, and grace for grace.

2. Contrast Moses and Jesus?

John 1:17 NKJV
For the law was given through Moses, but grace and truth came through Jesus Christ.

3. A. No man has done what?

   B. Who has declared God?

John 1:18 NKJV
No one has seen God at any time. The only begotten Son, who is in the bosom of the Father, He has declared Him.

4. A. Who is questioning John?

   B. What did they ask John?

John 1:19 NKJV
Now this is the testimony of John, when the Jews sent priests and Levites from Jerusalem to ask him, "Who are you?"

5. What did John say?

John 1:20 NKJV
He confessed, and did not deny, but confessed, "I am not the Christ."

6. A. What questions did they ask John?

   B. What was John's answer?

*John came in the spirit of Elijah. He was the natural son of Zacharias and Elizabeth. His job was to call for repentance (a heart change) and proclaim Christ's coming. He did not consider himself a prophet.

John 1:21 NKJV
And they asked him, "What then? Are you Elijah?" He said, "I am not." "Are you the Prophet?" And he answered, "No."

7. Then the priests and Levites asked what two questions?

John 1:22 NKJV
Then they said to him, "Who are you, that we may give an answer to those who sent us? What do you say about yourself?"

8. What was John's answer?

John 1:23 NKJV
He said: "I am 'The voice of one crying in the wilderness: "Make straight the way of the LORD,"' as the prophet Isaiah said."

9. Who sent the ones to question John?

John 1:24 NKJV
Now those who were sent were from the Pharisees.

10. What question did they ask?

John 1:25 NKJV
And they asked him, saying, "Why then do you baptize if you are not the Christ, nor Elijah, nor the Prophet?"

11. What was John's answer?

John 1:26 NKJV
John answered them, saying, "I baptize with water, but there stands One among you whom you do not know.

12. What did John say about Jesus?

John 1:27 NKJV
It is He who, coming after me, is preferred before me, whose sandal strap I am not worthy to loose."

Answers:
1. A. We have received God's fullness through Christ. B. Jesus's fullness is grace for grace.
2. Moses- Law (Old Testament); Jesus- Grace and truth (New Testament)
3. A. No man has seen or known God. B. Jesus declared God the Father.
4. John is being questioned by the Priests and Levites sent by Jews. They questioned "Who are you?"
5. John said, "I am not the Christ."
6. Are you Elijah or the prophet to come? John answered that he was not Elijah or the prophet.
7. Who are you? What do you say about yourself?
8. I am the voice of the one crying in the wilderness just like Isaiah said.
9. The Pharisees sent the ones to question John.
10. Why are you baptizing if you are not the Christ, Elijah, or the Prophet?
11. I baptize with water: but there stands one among you, whom you know not...
12. He is to come and is preferred before me, and I am not worthy to untie his shoes.

Outline:
- Jesus is the fullness.
- Jesus is grace and truth.
- Jesus gives New Testament grace for grace.
- John calls for repentance.
- John knows Jesus is greater than him.

Things to Ponder:
1. What thinking do I need to change so I may receive the fullness of grace and truth?

2. Is there prophecy over my life and how would I pray if I believed it?

3. Is there a burning passion in your heart to do something for Christ?

Challenge: Look up a few verses on grace and turn them into prayers. What would it look like to practice giving yourself grace today?

Write a prayer and ask God for the fullness of grace and truth and for a prophetic vision for your future. Write what you hear Him say, even if you are not sure about it.

Book of John

Day 4

The Lamb takes away the sins of the world.

Behold the Lamb of God! John 1:36

1. Where did John baptize?

John 1:28 NKJV
These things were done in Bethabara beyond the Jordan, where John was baptizing.

2. A. The next day who did John see coming towards him.

   B. What did John say?

*Jesus is the perfect sacrificial lamb to take away our sins.
John 1:29 NKJV
The next day John saw Jesus coming toward him, and said, "Behold! The Lamb of God who takes away the sin of the world!

3. What else did John say?

John 1:30 NKJV
This is He of whom I said, 'After me comes a Man who is preferred before me, for He was before me.

4. Did John know Jesus as Christ before this day?

John 1:31 NKJV
I did not know Him; but that He should be revealed to Israel, therefore I came baptizing with water."

5. A. Who bares record of Jesus being the Son of God?

B. How could John know Jesus was the Christ for certain?

John 1:32 NKJV
And John bore witness, saying, "I saw the Spirit descending from heaven like a dove, and He remained upon Him.

6. A. What was John's testimony as to how he knew that Jesus was the Christ?

B. What was John told that Jesus would baptize with?

John 1:33 NKJV
I did not know Him, but He who sent me to baptize with water said to me, 'Upon whom you see the Spirit descending, and remaining on Him, this is He who baptizes with the Holy Spirit.

7. John saw and bare record of what? "

John 1:34 NKJV
And I have seen and testified that this is the Son of God."

8. Who was with John the next day?

John 1:35 NKJV
Again, the next day, John stood with two of his disciples.

9. What did John say when he saw Jesus?

John 1:36 NKJV
And looking at Jesus as He walked, he said, "Behold the Lamb of God!"

10. What did the two disciples do?

Book of John

John 1:37 NKJV
The two disciples heard him speak, and they followed Jesus.

11. A. What did Jesus ask the two disciples?

   B. What did they answer?

John 1:38 NKJV
Then Jesus turned, and seeing them following, said to them, "What do you seek?" They said to Him, "Rabbi" (which is to say, when translated, Teacher), "where are You staying?"

12. A. What was Jesus's answer?

   B. Did they follow Jesus?

John 1:39 NKJV
He said to them, "Come and see." They came and saw where He was staying and remained with Him that day (now it was about the tenth hour).

Answers:
1. John baptized at Bethabara beyond Jordan.
2. A. The next day John saw Jesus coming. B. Behold the Lamb of God, which takes away the sin of the world.
3. Jesus came before me and is preferred above me.
4. No. "And I knew Him not."
5. A. John, bear record of Jesus being the Son of God. B. John knew Jesus was the Messiah because he saw the Holy Spirit descending from Heaven like a dove and abiding on Jesus.
6. A. The one who sent John to baptize told him that he would see the "...Spirit descending and remaining on him (the Christ) ..." B. John was told that Jesus will baptize with the Holy Ghost.
7. John bore record that Jesus is the Son of God.
8. The next day John was with two of his disciples.
9. When John saw Jesus he said, <u>Behold the Lamb of God!</u>
10. The two disciples followed Jesus now and not John the Baptist.
11. A. Jesus asked John's two disciples, "What seek you?" B. They answered, "Rabbi (Master) where do you live?"
12. A. Jesus answered, come, and see. B. Yes, they followed Jesus.

Outline:
- John was instructed by God to go and baptize with water.
- John knew the Messiah would come and He would recognize Him by the Spirit of God descending upon Him.
- John was to be a witness to identify the Messiah.
- John knew his disciples were good to follow Jesus and not him.
- John declares Jesus is the "Lamb of God."

Things to Ponder:

1. Have you experienced Jesus as your Messiah (Savior) who takes away your sins and makes you feel clean?

2. Are you following Jesus as your Master (teacher)?

3. Do you know how to tune your ear to hear the Holy Spirit?

Challenge: Make a mental note several times today and determine if you are filled with the fullness of joy (Psalm 16:11) or if there is something toxic taking up space in your life that needs renounced and rejected.

Book of John

Write your prayer and ask Jesus to baptize you with the baptism of the Holy Spirit. *Then, expect to feel a peace. This peace is the presence of the Holy Spirit. Wait for Him until he comes.

Angie Meadows

Day 5

Come...Follow me.

...we have found him, of whom Moses in the law, and the prophets, did write, Jesus of Nazareth, the son of Joseph. John 1:45

1. A. Who was one of the disciples that followed Jesus?

   B. Who was Andrew's brother?

John 1:40 NKJV
One of the two who heard John speak, and followed Him, was Andrew, Simon Peter's brother.

2. What did Andrew go and tell Peter?

John 1:41 NKJV
He first found his own brother Simon, and said to him, "We have found the Messiah" (which is translated, the Christ).

3. A. Who brought Peter to Jesus?

   B. What did Jesus rename Peter?

John 1:42 NKJV
And he brought him to Jesus. Now when Jesus looked at him, He said, "You are Simon the son of Jonah. You shall be called Cephas" (which is translated, A Stone).

4. A. Who did Jesus find?

Book of John

B. What did Jesus say to Philip?

John 1:43 NKJV
The following day Jesus wanted to go to Galilee, and He found Philip and said to him, "Follow Me."

5. Where was Philip from?

John 1:44 NKJV
Now Philip was from Bethsaida, the city of Andrew and Peter.

6. A. Who did Philip find?

B. What did Philip say to Nathanael?

John 1:45 NKJV
Philip found Nathanael and said to him, "We have found Him of whom Moses in the law, and also the prophets, wrote–Jesus of Nazareth, the son of Joseph."

7. A. What was Nathanael's reply?

B. What was Philip's reply?

*These men did not know that Jesus was born in Bethlehem and was raised in Nazareth.
John 1:46 NKJV
And Nathanael said to him, "Can anything good come out of Nazareth?" Philip said to him, "Come and see."

8. What did Jesus say about Nathanael?

*No deceit would mean that he had a pure heart with pure motives.
John 1:47 NKJV
Jesus saw Nathanael coming toward Him, and said of him, "Behold, an Israelite indeed, in whom is no deceit!"

9. A. Nathanael was surprised at Jesus' statement and said what?

B. What was Jesus's reply to Nathanael?

*Jesus describes a spiritual eye.
John 1:48 NKJV
Nathanael said to Him, "How do You know me?" Jesus answered and said to him, "Before Philip called you, when you were under the fig tree, I saw you."

10. What was Nathanael's reply?

John 1:49 NKJV
Nathanael answered and said to Him, "Rabbi, You are the Son of God! You are the King of Israel!"

11. What was Nathanael's reward for immediate faith?

John 1:50 NKJV
Jesus answered and said to him, "Because I said to you, 'I saw you under the fig tree,' do you believe? You will see greater things than these."

12. What is the greater things Nathanael shall see?

John 1:51 NKJV
And He said to him, "Most assuredly, I say to you, hereafter you shall see heaven open, and the angels of God ascending and descending upon the Son of Man."

Answers:

1. A. Andrew was one of the disciples that followed Jesus. B. Simon Peter was Andrew's brother.
2. Andrew told Peter that "we have found the Messiah (Christ)".
3. A. Andrew brought Peter to Jesus. B. Jesus renamed Peter "Cephas meaning a stone".
4. A. Jesus found Philip. B. Jesus told Philip to "Follow Me".
5. Philip was from the city of Bethsaida.
6. A. Philip found Nathanael. B. Philip told Nathanael that we have found the Messiah.
7. A. Nathanael's reply was "Can any good thing come out of Nazareth?" B. Philip's reply was to come and see for yourself.
8. Jesus said that Nathanael had no guile (deceit) in him.
9. A. Nathanael says how do you (Jesus) know me? B. Jesus responded, "I saw you under the fig tree before Phillip called you."
10. Nathanael immediately recognized Jesus as the Son of God, and the King of Israel?"
11. Nathanael's faith was immediately met with the gift of spiritual eyes. You shall see greater things than these.
12. Nathanael shall see angels ascending and descending upon the son of man.

Outline:

- Andrew recognized Jesus as the Messiah. His job was to introduce others to Jesus.
- Peter was renamed as a rock.
- Philip answered the call to "follow me".
- Nathanael was a man of no guile (deceit).
- Nathanael's received the gift of spiritual eyes.
- We have found four disciples now: Andrew, Peter, Philip, and Nathanael.

Things to Ponder:

1. Can you recognize noise in your heart and mind that isn't pure?

2. Is it exciting for you to introduce others to Jesus? If not, ask the Lord what is hindering you from acting on your beliefs?

3. Ask God to give you a new name and listen for it. What did you hear?

Jesus	John
• Fullness	• I am not the Christ
• Grace and truth	• Calls for repentance (heart change)
• Jesus declares the Father	• Witness to identify the Messiah
• Takes away sin	• Voice crying in the wilderness
• Baptizes with the Spirit	• Baptizes with water
• Preferred	• Spirit of Elijah

Challenge: Today, determine on a scale of 1-10 (10 being the most) how much work it would take to move everything that causes you to be emotionally imbalanced out of your heart. Validate the feeling or circumstance but release it to God and give it no place of power of you. Instead, embrace those things that are pure and give you peace.

Write a prayer and ask the Lord to open your spiritual eyes.

John 2

The beginning of miracles.

His mother said to the servants, "Whatever He says to you, do it." John 2:5

Day 6

1. What was the event?

    B. Where was it?

    C. Who was there?

John 2:1 NKJV
On the third day there was a wedding in Cana of Galilee, and the mother of Jesus was there.

2. Who was called to the marriage?

John 2:2 NKJV
Now both Jesus and His disciples were invited to the wedding.

3. When they wanted wine, what did Jesus' mother, Mary, say to Him?

John 2:3 NKJV

And when they ran out of wine, the mother of Jesus said to Him, "They have no wine."

4. What was Jesus's reply to Mary?

John 2:4 NKJV
Jesus said to her, "Woman, what does your concern have to do with Me? My hour has not yet come."

5. What did Mary say?

Mary's last recorded words.
John 2:5 NKJV
His mother said to the servants, "Whatever He says to you, do it."

6. How many waterpots were there?

*This would represent 100-200 gallons.
John 2:6 NKJV
Now there were set there six waterpots of stone, according to the manner of purification of the Jews, containing twenty or thirty gallons apiece.

7. A. What was Jesus' request to the servants?

  B. How full were they to fill the pots?

John 2:7 NKJV
Jesus said to them, "Fill the waterpots with water." And they filled them up to the brim.

8. What did Jesus tell them to do?

John 2:8 NKJV
And He said to them, "Draw some out now, and take it to the master of the feast." And they took it.

9. What did the governor of the feast do when he tasted the wine?

John 2:9 NKJV
When the master of the feast had tasted the water that was made wine and did not know where it came from (but the servants who had drawn the water knew), the master of the feast called the bridegroom.

10. What did the governor say to the bridegroom?

John 2:10 NKJV
And he said to him, "Every man at the beginning sets out the good wine, and when the guests have well drunk, then the inferior. You have kept the good wine until now!"

11. A. Why was this event significant?

　B. What was the purpose of this miracle and all miracles?

　C. What did this do in the disciples' hearts?

John 2:11 NKJV
This beginning of signs Jesus did in Cana of Galilee and manifested His glory; and His disciples believed in Him.

Answers:
1. A. The event was a wedding. B. It was at Cana of Galilee. C. Mary, Jesus' mother was there.
2. Jesus and His disciples were invited to the wedding.
3. They have no wine.
4. Woman, what does that have to do with Me? Mine hour is not come.
5. Whatsoever He says to you, do it.
6. There were six waterpots.
7. A. Fill the waterpots with water. B. Fill the pots to the brim.
8. Draw out now and take it to the governor of the feast.
9. The governor of the feast called the bridegroom.
10. Every man at the beginning set forth good wine; and when men have well drunk, then that which is worse: but you have kept the good wine until now.
11. A. This was significant because it marked the beginning of the miracles of Jesus. B. It was to manifest Jesus' glory. C. It caused them to believe on Him.

Outline:
- This was Jesus's first miracle.

- It was a wedding.
- The location was Cana of Galilee
- The mother of Jesus initiated the miracle.
- The problem was that the wine ran out.
- Mary, Jesus's mother, instructs the servants to do whatever He says.
- Mary came to Jesus with the problem of the hosts. She interceded for them.
- The servants obeyed everything Jesus said to do.
- The Governor was impressed. The best was saved for last.
- The first purpose of miracles is to manifest the glory of God through Jesus.
- The second purpose was to instill belief in the hearts of His disciples.

Thoughts to Ponder:

1. Why would Jesus do a miracle that He even said He didn't intend to do?

2. Could it have to do with His relationship with His momma?

3. Do you have a close enough friendship with Jesus to be comfortable to ask for what your friends need?

Challenge: Pray the prayer in Ephesians 3:16-19. What would the fullness of God look like in your life. Hint: The answer is in the next verse: Ephesians 3:20.

Write a prayer: What is it that you need to ask Jesus to do for you or your friends? James 4:2 says we have not because we ask not?

Day 7

Jesus is the temple.

But He was speaking of the temple of His body. John 2:21
NKJV

1. A. Where did Jesus go from here?

   B. Who went with him?

John 2:12 NKJV
After this He went down to Capernaum, He, His mother, His brothers, and His disciples; and they did not stay there many days.

2. A. Where did they go next?

   B. What was happening in Jerusalem?

John 2:13 NKJV
Now the Passover of the Jews was at hand, and Jesus went up to Jerusalem.

3. Who was in the temple?

*The Jews were overcharging for the animals and for foreign currency exchange in the temple money.
John 2:14 NKJV
And He found in the temple those who sold oxen and sheep and doves, and the money changers doing business.

4. How did Jesus respond to this dishonesty in His Father's temple?

John 2:15 NKJV

Book of John

When He had made a whip of cords, He drove them all out of the temple, with the sheep and the oxen, and poured out the changers' money and overturned the tables.

5. What did Jesus say to them?

John 2:16 NKJV
And He said to those who sold doves, "Take these things away! Do not make My Father's house a house of merchandise!"

6. Then what verse did the disciples remember?

John 2:17 NKJV
Then His disciples remembered that it was written, "Zeal for Your house has eaten Me up."

7. What were the Jews looking for?

John 2:18 NKJV
So, the Jews answered and said to Him, "What sign do You show to us, since You do these things?"

8. What was Jesus' answer?

*This is the one and only true sign (the resurrection) that Jesus was the Messiah.
John 2:19 NKJV
Jesus answered and said to them, "Destroy this temple, and in three days I will raise it up."

9. What temple did the Jews think He was referring to?

*Unbelief closes the eyes of understanding.
John 2:20 NKJV
Then the Jews said, "It has taken forty-six years to build this temple, and will You raise it up in three days?"

10. What does this Scripture confirm?

John 2:21 NKJV
But He was speaking of the temple of His body.

11. For whose benefit did Jesus say these words?

John 2:22 NKJV
Therefore, when He had risen from the dead, His disciples remembered that He had said this to them; and they believed the Scripture and the word which Jesus had said.

12. During the Passover feast what caused many to believe in His name?

John 2:23 NKJV
Now when He was in Jerusalem at the Passover, during the feast, many believed in His name when they saw the signs which He did.

13. What does this mean, "Jesus did not commit Himself unto them...?"

John 2:24 NKJV
But Jesus did not commit Himself to them, because He knew all men,

14. Why did Jesus not need someone else to tell Him about the heart condition of these men?

John 2:25 NKJV
and had no need that anyone should testify of man, for He knew what was in man.

Answers:

1. A. Jesus went to Capernaum. B. His mother, brethren, and disciples went with him.
2. A. They went to Jerusalem. B. The Jew's Passover was happening.
3. Those who sold oxen, sheep and doves, and the changers of money were in the temple.

4. He made a whip of small cords, and he drove the sheep and the oxen out of the temple. He poured out the changers' money and overthrew their tables.
5. Take these things out of here, make not my Father's house a house of merchandise.
6. The zeal of thine house has eaten me up.
7. The Jews were looking for a sign.
8. Destroy this temple, and in three days I will raise it up. He was referring to his body as the temple.
9. Their elaborate temple that took 46 years to build. They people scoffed at Jesus.
10. That he was speaking of the temple of his body.
11. It was said for the disciple's sake so they would understand and believe when he was raised from the dead.
12. They saw the miracles he did, and many believed.
13. It most likely means he did not trust them.
14. Jesus had full knowledge and could correctly judge a man's heart. Unredeemed flesh cannot be trusted.

Outline:
- The temple should be kept pure and without dishonest people using it for dishonest gain against the innocent people coming to worship God.
- Zeal for righteousness was Jesus's rule.
- Jesus is the temple. He was crucified and resurrected in three days.
- The benefit of Jesus's teaching was for the disciples to increase their belief later after the crucifixion and resurrection.

Things to Ponder:
1. What was the one and only true sign that Jesus was the Messiah?

2. Can Jesus fully trust your heart motives?

3. Jesus addressed unbelief in every chapter of John. Is there an area of unbelief in your life that you need to release to God? You will find unbelief in areas of suffering that you are trying to fix, or control that need surrendered.

Challenge: What area in life do you feel powerless over?

Do you have a person or circumstance in life that you have not surrendered to God?

Write a prayer and offer the Lord your unbelief and ask him to teach you to believe today?

John 3

Born again.

Except a man be born again, he cannot see the kingdom of God. John 3:3

Day 8

1. Who was Nicodemus?

John 3:1 NKJV
There was a man of the Pharisees named Nicodemus, a ruler of the Jews.

2. What did Nicodemus say to Jesus?

*Rabbi means teacher of the Jewish law.
John 3:2 NKJV
This man came to Jesus by night and said to Him, "Rabbi, we know that You are a teacher come from God; for no one can do these signs that You do unless God is with him."

3. What reward do we receive if we are born again?

John 3:3 NKJV
Jesus answered and said to him, "Most assuredly, I say to you, unless one is born again, he cannot see the kingdom of God."

4. Did Nicodemus understand how to be "born again"?

John 3:4 NKJV
Nicodemus said to Him, "How can a man be born when he is old? Can he enter a second time into his mother's womb and be born?"

5. What does it mean to be born of the water and the spirit?

*There is a death to fleshly self, so that your spiritual self may come to life. John 12:24
*Buried in Christ by baptism into death and raised in newness of life. Romans 6:4; Colossians 2:12
*Are you able to drink of the baptism Jesus was baptized with? Matthew 20:22
*Baptism of repentance Mark 1:4
John 3:5 NKJV Jesus answered, "Most assuredly, say to you, unless one is born of water and the Spirit, he cannot enter the kingdom of God.

6. What is Jesus saying?

John 3:6 NKJV
That which is born of the flesh is flesh, and that which is born of the Spirit is spirit.

7. What is Jesus saying?

John 3:7 NKJV
Do not marvel that I said to you, 'You must be born again.

8. A. Who can hear the wind blow?

   B. Who can hear the Spirit's voice? (See Romans 8:1-13)

John 3:8 NKJV
The wind blows where it wishes, and you hear the sound of it, but cannot tell where it comes from and where it goes. So is everyone who is born of the Spirit."

9. Did Nicodemus understand?

John 3:9 NKJV
Nicodemus answered and said to Him, "How can these things be?"

Answers:
1. Nicodemus was a Pharisee and a ruler of the Jews.
2. Rabbi, we know that you are a teacher come from God: for no man can do these miracles that you do except God be with Him.
3. Born again believers can see the kingdom of God.
4. No, Nicodemus didn't know the difference between physical and spiritual birth.
5. Born of the water may mean washed in the Word. Born of the Spirit would be evidence of the Holy Spirit in your life.
6. Any man born of the flesh will walk in sin and any man born of the Spirit walk in the Spirit.
7. Don't think being born again is too great a thing to happen.
8. A. Every person can hear or feel the wind blow. B. A born-again believer can hear the Spirit's voice.
9. No, Nicodemus did not understand.

Outline:
- Nicodemus calls Jesus, teacher.
- A born-again person will experience the kingdom of God.
- There is a physical birth and a spiritual birth.
- There is a kingdom of God we can see with our spiritual eyes when we are reborn.
- Effects of the Spirit can be seen like the effects of the wind can be seen.

Things to Ponder:
1. Have you been born again?

2. Born again believers will be growing and not stagnant. They will be seeking to draw closer to God and mature. How are you growing and maturing?

3. Compared to ten years ago, are you a stronger believer or weaker?

Challenge: When we see something that is irritating in another person, it is something that the Holy Spirit is magnifying in front of us so we can get the plank out of our own eye and not pick at the speck in our brother's eye. Matthew 7:5

Write a prayer and ask for the Spirit to show you what areas in your life needs healed and matured.

Book of John

Day 9

Belief is Eternal Life

...that whoever believes in Him should not perish but have eternal life. John 3:15

1. Did Jesus expect that a teacher of the law should understand salvation?

John 3:10 NKJV
Jesus answered and said to him, "Are you the teacher of Israel, and do not know these things?

2. Was Nicodemus able to understand and receive what Jesus was saying?

John 3:11 NKJV
Most assuredly, I say to you, we speak what we know and testify what we have seen, and you do not receive our witness.

3. What does it take to understand heavenly things?

John 3:12 NKJV If I have told you earthly things and you do not believe, how will you believe if I tell you heavenly things?

4. What event is this verse testifying?

John 3:13 NKJV
No one has ascended to heaven but He who came down from heaven, that is, the Son of Man who is in heaven.

5. A. Do you remember the story of Moses and the brazen serpent on the cross?

B. How is this an analogy for us with Christ?

The Israelites were in the desert and were dying because of poisonous snake bites. Moses prayed and God told him to make an image of a serpent and put it on a cross and if the people would just look upon it, they would not die. This is a visual Old Testament picture of the need for Jesus to die on the cross to save us from our sins. (Numbers 21:9)
* Now sin has no power over us when we look to the cross of Jesus Christ!

John 3:14 NKJV And as Moses lifted up the serpent in the wilderness, even so must the Son of Man be lifted up,

6. Why did Jesus come to earth?

John 3:15 NKJV
that whoever believes in Him should not perish but have eternal life.

7. A. Why would God sacrifice His only Son?

B. What is the will of God for you in this verse?

John 3:16 NKJV
For God so loved the world that He gave His only begotten Son, that whoever believes in Him should not perish but have everlasting life.

8. Why did God send His Son into the world?

John 3:17 NKJV
For God did not send His Son into the world to condemn the world, but that the world through Him might be saved.

9. A. How does it describe one who believes on Jesus?

B. How does this verse describe one who doesn't believe?

John 3:18 NKJV
"He who believes in Him is not condemned; but he who does not believe is condemned already, because he has not believed in the name of the only begotten Son of God.
*It is belief in Jesus that saves.

Answers:
1. Yes, Jesus expected a teacher of the law to have insight into spiritual things.
2. No, Nicodemus couldn't understand at this time.
3. It takes <u>believing</u> before the eyes of your understanding are opened.
4. It is speaking about Jesus's divinity and His descending and ascending from heaven and back to heaven.
5. A. All we must do is look to Jesus. Sin was the serpent. B. The cross represents the perfect sacrifice for our sin.
6. Jesus came to die for our sins and redeem us so we could have eternal life.
7. A. God loved us and wanted us to have a way to be restored. God's perfect will is to give us the gift of eternal life.
8. God doesn't want to condemn the world but wants to save the world through His Son.
9. A. A believer is not condemned. B. A non-believer is condemned by default.

Outline:
- Spiritual maturity will have insight into spiritual things.
- Even our teachers are struggling to understand when God is doing a new thing.
- Jesus is God.
- The cross is the power of forgiveness to wash away the sting of sin.
- The gift is eternal life.
- It is God's will to save the world.
- A believer is not condemned.

Things to Ponder:
1. Anxiety signals unbelief. Quietly trusting in the Lord and his unseen hand, leads to strength (Isaiah 30:15b). Take one thing that causes you unnecessary stress or anxiety and release it to the Lord.

2. Move fear of the future to the altar. Lord, I give you.... Lord, I release to you....

3. Ask for forgiveness for not believing. A temporal focus struggles to believe. An eternal focus sees through spiritual eyes (2 Corinthians 4:18).

Challenge: Five time today recognize where your affections are centered and recalibrate to consistently set your affections on things above (Colossians 3:2).

Write a prayer and confess any unbelief and ask the Lord to help you believe.

Book of John

Day 10

Jesus is the light!

...that the light has come into the world... John 3:19

1. A. What does it mean when it says this is the condemnation?

    B. Who is the light?

*I don't have to stay in condemnation.
John 3:19 NKJV
And this is the condemnation, that the light has come into the world, and men loved darkness rather than light, because their deeds were evil.

2. Will an evil man come to the light?

John 3:20 NKJV
For everyone practicing evil hates the light and does not come to the light, lest his deeds should be exposed.

3. A. Who comes to the light?

    B. What kind of deeds will this man do?

John 3:21 NKJV
But he who does the truth comes to the light, that his deeds may be clearly seen, that they have been done in God."

4. A. Where did Jesus and His disciples go next?

B. What were they doing?

John 3:22 NKJV
After these things Jesus and His disciples came into the land of Judea, and there He remained with them and baptized.

5. What was John the Baptist still doing?

John 3:23 NKJV
Now John also was baptizing in Aenon near Salim because there was much water there. And they came and were baptized.

6. What will happen to John the Baptist?

John 3:24 NKJV
For John had not yet been thrown into prison.

7. What was the question that arose between John the Baptist' disciples and the Jews?

John 3:25 NKJV
Then there arose a dispute between some of John's disciples and the Jews about purification.

8. What were they saying to John?

John 3:26 NKJV
And they came to John and said to him, "Rabbi, He who was with you beyond the Jordan, to whom you have testified-behold, He is baptizing, and all are coming to Him!"

9. Is John jealous?

Book of John

John 3:27 NKJV
John answered and said, "A man can receive nothing unless it has been given to him from heaven.

10. Does John know who he is?

John 3:28 NKJV
You yourselves bear me witness, that I said, 'I am not the Christ,' but, 'I have been sent before Him.

11. What picture does John use to express his feelings towards Jesus?

John 3:29 NKJV
He who has the bride is the bridegroom; but the friend of the bridegroom, who stands and hears him, rejoices greatly because of the bridegroom's voice. Therefore, this joy of mine is fulfilled.

12. Now what is John saying to the people? *

*When we come to Jesus our self-will must decrease so that the will of God may increase in our hearts.
John 3:30 NKJV
He must increase, but I must decrease.

13. A. Who is John referring to that has come from above?

B. Who is from earth?

* John is making a distinction between himself and Jesus.
John 3:31 NKJV
He who comes from above is above all; he who is of the earth is earthly and speaks of the earth. He who comes from heaven is above all.

Answers:
1. A. Those who are willingly abiding in darkness are willingly staying under condemnation. B. Jesus is the light.

2. No, he won't come to the light because his deeds would be reproved or exposed.

3. A. The ones that come to the light love truth. B. A person walking in the truth will have deeds that are of God.

4. Jesus and the disciples went to Judaea. They were baptizing.

5. John the Baptist was still baptizing.

6. John will be cast into prison.

7. The dispute was about which is the best way to purify a man from sin.

8. They said, Jesus and His disciples are baptizing, and everyone is going to them.

9. No, John is not jealous. He acknowledges that everything he has comes from God.

10. Yes, John knows he is the forerunner to Christ.

11. John pictures Jesus as the bridegroom and himself as the "friend of the bridegroom".

12. As the Spirit increases, the flesh will die.

13. Jesus comes from above. John is from the earth.

Outline:
- Jesus is the light. Light exposes our deeds... good and bad.
- Those who love evil will hide their deeds in darkness.
- John is the earthly forerunner, and the bridegroom's friend.
- John will soon die for his message.
- John acknowledges that all he has received has come from heaven.
- John says to watch the bridegroom fulfills his joy.

Things to Ponder:
1. Many will never read their Bibles, but they will read you. Are you a living letter to enlighten the path to eternal life for others? 2 Corinthians 3:3

2. Who in your life could you come along side and support in their ministry? Write, text, or call them and give them words of encouragement.

Book of John

Challenge: Do you live a transparent life or are you hiding anything? If so, confess and turn away from sin, that you can be cleansed. 1 John 1:9

Write a prayer asking God for the strength to be the person He wants you to become?

Angie Meadows

Day 11

Belief is Everlasting Life

He who believes in the Son has everlasting life; John 3:36

1. Had no man received Jesus' testimony?

John 3:32 NKJV
And what He has seen and heard, that He testifies; and no one receives His testimony.

2. If we receive Jesus's testimony, what are we saying?

John 3:33 NKJV
He who has received His testimony has certified that God is true.

3. A. Who did God send?

    B. Does God limit His Spirit on Jesus?

John 3:34 NKJV
For He whom God has sent speaks the words of God, for God does not give the Spirit by measure.

4. What does this verse confirm?

John 3:35 NKJV

The Father loves the Son and has given all things into His hand.

5. A. What blessing do we receive if we believe in Jesus as our Savior?

   B. What two things do we receive if we believe not?

John 3:36 NKJV
He who believes in the Son has everlasting life; and he who does not believe the Son shall not see life, but the wrath of God abides on him."

Answers:
1. Up to this point in His ministry, it could have been true that no one understood He was the Messiah.
2. Receiving the testimony of Christ is saying God is true.
3. God sent His son, Jesus. No, God gave Jesus His Spirit without limits.
4. This verse confirms that God loved Jesus and gave Him all things.
5. A. Jesus gives us everlasting life. B. We will not see life and will have the wrath of God abiding on us.

Outline:
- Reading the gospels and asking the Holy Spirit to strengthen our belief is priority for growth as a believer.
- If we can be one with Christ, we can also have the Spirit without measure. This would be possible as we receive more of Him and less of us.
- If Jesus has been given all things, we will have all we need in Him.
- If the Lord doesn't provide it, we don't need it.
- Light and life of Jesus will bring us hope and fill us with joy and peace, and we will abound in the Holy Spirit. Romans 15:13

Things to Ponder:
1. What part of your life are you wrestling with that feels like the wrath of God? Is this a fleshly part that needs to be given up?

2. Is there a toxic person that blocks your growing in Christ that needs boundaries or distance?

3. What would it look like if you surrendered an area of difficulty in your life and settled yourself internally to simply believe God will guide you in this journey?

Challenge: Can you accept that the Lord can redeem the sins others did against you or even your past sin/regrets and take what was meant for evil and make it good? Genesis 50:20

Write a prayer and ask for something you don't have that you need. James 4:2b

John 4

The woman at the well

"Give Me a drink." John 4:7

Day 12

1. Who heard that Jesus was baptizing more that John?

John 4:1 NKJV
Therefore, when the Lord knew that the Pharisees had heard that Jesus made and baptized more disciples than John.

2. Did Jesus Himself baptize?

John 4:2 NKJV
(though Jesus Himself did not baptize, but His disciples),

3. Where did they leave from and where did they go?

John 4:3 NKJV
He left Judea and departed again to Galilee.

4. What city did they go through?

Book of John

John 4:4 NKJV
But He needed to go through Samaria.

5. A. What was the name of the place in Samaria?

   B. Why was it significant?

* Jesus and His disciples stopped at Jacob's well.
John 4:5 NKJV
So, he came to a city of Samaria which is called Sychar, near the plot of ground that Jacob gave to his son Joseph.

6. A. Did Jesus have a physical body and weary like we do?

   B. What time was it?

John 4:6 NKJV
Now Jacob's well was there. Jesus, therefore, being wearied from His journey, sat thus by the well. It was about the sixth hour.

7. A. Who did Jesus speak to at the well?

   B. What did He say to her?

   C. Why did Jesus need her to give Him a drink?

John 4:7 NKJV
A woman of Samaria came to draw water. Jesus said to her, "Give Me a drink."

8. Where were the disciples?

John 4:8 NKJV
For His disciples had gone away into the city to buy food.

Answers:
1. The Pharisees' heard Jesus was baptizing more than John.
2. No, his disciples did the baptizing.
3. They left Judaea and went to Galilee.
4. They needed to go through Samaria.
5. A. Sychar was the name of the place in Samaria. B. It is significant because it is the ground that Jacob gave to his son Joseph.
6. Yes, Jesus had a physical body with limitations. It was noon.
7. A, Jesus spoke to a woman. B. He asked her for a drink. C. She had a physical container to draw water from the well and he did not.
8. The disciples went into the city to buy food.

Outline:
- Disciples were baptizing more than John.
- Jacob's well was a place known for blessing.
- Jesus had physical limitations and needed to sleep and eat like we do.
- Most women went to the well for water in the morning and to socialize. This woman wasn't liked enough to come with the other women.
- Jesus intentionally begins a conversation with a woman who was a Samaritan.

Things to Ponder:
1. Who is despised in your eyes (maybe with prejudice)? (Sometimes it is an animal or an object we despise.)

2. How could you show kindness to someone who is bitter towards you?

3. Are there places you avoid so you can avoid the rejections (or feelings of rejection) from others?

Challenge: Today or someday soon when the opportunity presents itself, give someone a drink in the name of love (Jesus).

Book of John

Write a prayer and ask God to show you any prejudice He would like you to correct.

Day 13

Jesus breaks social rules.

I ... will become in him... a fountain of water springing up into everlasting life. John 4:14

1. What did the woman say?

John 4:9 NKJV
Then the woman of Samaria said to Him, "How is it that You, being a Jew, ask a drink from me, a Samaritan woman?" For Jews have no dealings with Samaritans.

2. What was Jesus' answer?

John 4:10 NKJV
Jesus answered and said to her, "If you knew the gift of God, and who it is who says to you, 'Give Me a drink,' you would have asked Him, and He would have given you living water."

3. Does the woman understand the difference between physical and spiritual water?

John 4:11 NKJV
The woman said to Him, "Sir, you have nothing to draw with, and the well is deep. Where then do You get that living water?

4. Who does she consider great?

John 4:12 NKJV
Are You greater than our father Jacob, who gave us the well, and drank from it himself, as well as his sons and his livestock?"

Book of John

5. After we drink physical water will we be thirsty again?

John 4:13 NKJV
Jesus answered and said to her, "Whoever drinks of this water will thirst again,

6. A. What kind of water will Jesus give us?

   B. This well of water will develop into what?

*A spring or fountain is a continual source of life.
John 4:14 NKJV
but whoever drinks of the water that I shall give him will never thirst. But the water that I shall give him will become in him a fountain of water springing up into everlasting life."

7. Is the woman thinking in physical or spiritual terms?

John 4:15 NKJV
The woman said to Him, "Sir, give me this water, that I may not thirst, nor come here to draw."

8. What is Jesus doing?

John 4:16 NKJV
Jesus said to her, "Go, call your husband, and come here."

9. A. What was the woman's answer?

   B. What was Jesus' reply?

John 4:17 NKJV

The woman answered and said, "I have no husband." Jesus said to her, "You have well said, 'I have no husband,'

10. Does Jesus allow this woman to be superficial?

*Can't be superficial with Jesus, He already knows.
John 4:18 NKJV
for you have had five husbands, and the one whom you now have is not your husband; in that you spoke truly."*

11. What does the woman perceive?

*John 4:19 NKJV
The woman said to Him, "Sir, I perceive that You are a prophet.*

Answers:
1. How is it that you, being a Jew, ask a drink of me, which am a woman of Samaria?
2. If you knew the gift of God...you would have asked of Him, and He would have given you living water.
3. No, she, like Nicodemus doesn't understand the difference between the physical and the spiritual.
4. The Samaritan woman considers their forefather, Jacob, great.
5. Yes, the physical body will need constant sustaining.
6. Jesus gives living water that develops into a well spring of water.
7. Her thinking is in the physical realm. She doesn't want to return to the well in the heat of the day.
8. He is getting to the root of her problem, so He can give her living water.
9. The woman answered I have no husband. Jesus responded that is true.
10. No, He tells her the depths of her past.
11. The woman perceives that Jesus is a prophet with wisdom.

Outline:
- Jesus breaks social rules and speaks to a Samaritan woman.
- There is a difference between physical and spiritual water.
- Water represents life.
- The spiritual life needs the same consistent care that the physical body needs.
- Jesus continually fills us with the well spring of the water of life.

Things to Ponder:
1. What would it feel like to drink living water throughout your day?

2. What will it look like when God activates your spiritual ear?

3. What would it look like to nurture your spirit with consistent care?

Challenge: Lay quietly upon your bed at night and drop into your spirit until you feel the presence of the Holy Spirit warm your heart. This will take quieting all the noise of the day and releasing it and tuning into God. Psalm 4:4

Write a prayer by turning around Psalm 61:7 Asked the Lord to enthrone you in His presence forever. Draw a picture of what that would look like.

Day 14

Worship is spiritual.

...the true worshipers will worship the Father in spirit and truth. John 4:23

1. What is the woman doing?

John 4:20 NKJV
Our Fathers worshiped on this mountain, and you Jews say that in Jerusalem is the place where one ought to worship."

2. Who does Jesus say is right, the Samaritans or the Jews?

John 4:21 NKJV
Jesus said to her, "Woman, believe Me, the hour is coming when you will neither on this mountain, nor in Jerusalem, worship the Father.

3. Can we be sincere and worship and misunderstand truth?

John 4:22 NKJV
You worship what you do not know; we know what we worship, for salvation is of the Jews.

4. What does Jesus say about true worship?

John 4:23 NKJV
But the hour is coming, and now is, when the true worshipers will worship the Father in spirit and truth; for the Father is seeking such to worship Him.

5. What does Jesus say about true worshippers?

John 4:24 NKJV

Book of John

God is Spirit, and those who worship Him must worship in spirit and truth."

6. A. What does the woman say they are looking for?

   B. What will Messiah do?

John 4:25 NKJV
The woman said to Him, "I know that Messiah is coming" (who is called Christ). "When He comes, He will <u>tell us all things</u>."

7. What did Jesus reveal to her?

*He revealed His identity as Messiah to an immoral woman.
John 4:26 NKJV
Jesus said to her, "I who speak to you am He."

8. Do the disciples have the confidence in this situation to question Jesus about His actions?

* It was custom not to deal with Samaritans or for a Rabbi to speak to woman in public.
John 4:27 NKJV
And at this point His disciples came, and they marveled that He talked with a woman; yet no one said, "What do You seek?" or "Why are You talking with her?"

9. What did the woman do next?

John 4:28 NKJV
The woman then left her waterpot, went her way into the city, and said to the men,

10. What was the woman saying to the people of the city?

John 4:29 NKJV
"Come, see a Man who told me all things that I ever did. Could this be the Christ?"

11. Did the people of the city listen to the woman at the well?

John 4:30 NKJV
Then they went out of the city and came to Him.

Answers:
1. Possibly diverting the subject so she doesn't get too uncomfortable.
2. Neither are right.
3. Yes, Jesus explains we can worship wrong.
4. True worshippers worship the Father.
5. They will worship in Spirit and truth because God is a Spirit.
6. A. They are looking for the Messiah. B. Messiah will tell them all things.
7. Jesus revealed that He is the Messiah.
8. No, the disciples didn't have the confidence to ask Jesus about His actions.
9. The woman went into the city.
10. She was calling others to come and see the Messiah.
11. Yes, the people listened to her.

Outline:
- True worshippers learn to activate their spirit to worship the Father.
- Sincerely seeking God will bring more revelation and truth.
- We are never too sinful or lost to be introduced to the Messiah.
- You are never too low for Jesus to speak to you.
- You are never too sinful to tell others about what Jesus has done for you.

Things to Ponder:
1. What things do you do to procrastinate from dealing with the things in your life that hurt? Are your coping skills healthy or unhealthy?

2. Why would we need to worship the Father in the Spirit?

3. Is there an area in your life where you feel guilt and shame that needs released?

Challenge: Many start out well but do not have the strength of character to finish well. How do you plan to finish well in the race of life? 2 Timothy 4:7

Write a prayer and ask God to empower you to walk in the Spirit so you will not fulfill the lust of the flesh. Galatians 5:16

Day 15

The Harvest is Ripe!

... that both he who sows, and he who reaps may rejoice together.
John 4:36

3. What did the disciples say to Jesus?

John 4:31 NKJV
In the meantime, His disciples urged Him, saying, "Rabbi, eat."

4. What kind of food (physical or spiritual)?

John 4:32 NKJV
But He said to them, "I have food to eat of which you do not know."

5. Are the disciples confused, again?

John 4:33 NKJV
Therefore, the disciples said to one another, "Has anyone brought Him anything to eat?"

6. What was Jesus' meat or His delight?

John 4:34 NKJV
Jesus said to them, My food is to do the will of Him who sent Me, and to finish His work.

7. Is this harvest physical or spiritual?

John 4:35 NKJV
Do you not say, 'There are still four months and then comes the harvest'? Behold, I say to you, lift up your eyes and look at the fields, for they are already white for harvest!

Book of John

8. What did Jesus say we are reaping?

John 4:36 NKJV
And he who reaps receives wages, and gathers fruit for eternal life, that both he who sows, and he who reaps may rejoice together.

9. Does the person who sows always reap?

John 4:37 NKJV
For in this the saying is true: 'One sows, and another reaps.'

10. What's our job?

*Seasoned Christians can discern when a person is ready for salvation.
John 4:38 NKJV
I sent you to reap that for which you have not labored; others have labored, and you have entered into their labors."*

11. What are the key words in this verse?

John 4:39 NKJV
And many of the Samaritans of that city <u>believed</u> in Him because of the word of the woman who testified, "He told me all that I ever did."

12. Why did Jesus stay in Samaria two more days?

* It is God that prepares the hearts of people to receive good seed. It is us that need the spiritual eyes to be fishers of men. Matthew 4:19
John 4:40 NKJV
So, when the Samaritans had come to Him, they urged Him to stay with them; and He stayed there two days.

13. Did these despised Samaritans believe on Jesus?

John 4:41 NKJV
And many more believed because of His own word.

14. Did they believe even more after they heard Jesus speak?

John 4:42 NKJV
Then they said to the woman, "Now we believe, not because of what you said, for we ourselves have heard Him and we know that this is indeed the Christ, the Savior of the world."

15. Where did Jesus go next?

John 4:43 NKJV
Now after the two days He departed from there and went to Galilee.

Answers:
1. The disciples said, "Rabbi (or Master), eat."
2. Jesus spoke of spiritual food.
3. Often, the disciples are confused when Jesus speaks spiritually.
4. Jesus's meat was the satisfaction of converting the Samaritans. This Jesus indicates is the Father's work.
5. The harvest Jesus speaks about is spiritual.
6. We are reaping eternal life.
7. No, some sow and others may reap.
8. Our job is to see spiritually and reap a ripe harvest when it is ready.
9. Believed and testified are the key words.
10. The people urged Jesus to stay.
11. Yes, they believed when they listened to Jesus.
12. Yes, hearing Jesus speak solidified their belief.
13. Jesus and His disciples went to Galilee.

Outline:
- Jesus's disciples were urging Him to eat food. They cared about supporting Him physically.
- Spiritual food is to delight in doing God's work.
- Opened spiritual eyes see a spiritual harvest ready to be reaped.
- There is a sowing of a seed for eternal life.
- There is a reaping of others for eternal life.
- There is a rejoicing when we see a spiritual harvest.
- Belief is a key word throughout the book of John.
- Our spirits can recognize truth when it is spoken if we are spiritually minded.

Things to Ponder:
1. If your spirit is alive, what might be your delight?

2. Who in your life is ready and eager to listen and be discipled by you? Is there a child that needs to be nurtured in the Word?

3. Who is your mentor that loves to feed into you spiritually?

Challenge: We all need an Apostle Paul to disciple us. A Barnabas to cheer us on and a Timothy to mentor and encourage. Can you name your support mentor, encourager, and your disciple(s)?

Write a prayer: ask God for loyal and devoted friends that are like-minded.

Day 16

Jesus the Miracle Worker!

Jesus said to him, "Go your way; your son lives." John 4:50

1. What principle is spoken in this Scripture?

John 4:44 NKJV
For Jesus Himself testified that a prophet has no honor in his own country.

2. Why did the Galileans receive Jesus?

John 4:45 NKJV
So, when He came to Galilee, the Galileans received Him, having seen all the things He did in Jerusalem at the feast; for they also had gone to the feast.

3. Why did the nobleman come to Jesus for a miracle for his son?

John 4:46 NKJV
So, Jesus came again to Cana of Galilee where He had made the water wine. And there was a certain nobleman whose son was sick at Capernaum.

4. What's going on in this verse?

John 4:47 NKJV
When he heard that Jesus had come out of Judea into Galilee, he went to Him and implored Him to come down and heal his son, for he was at the point of death.

5. What are the benefits of others seeing signs and wonders?

John 4:48 NKJV

Then Jesus said to him, "Unless you people see signs and wonders, you will by no means believe."

6. How sick was his son?

John 4:49 NKJV
The nobleman said to Him, "Sir, come down before my child dies!"

7. How did Jesus heal the son?

John 4:50 NKJV
Jesus said to him, "Go your way; your son lives." So, the man believed the word that Jesus spoke to him, and he went his way.

8. What did the man's servant say to Him?

John 4:51 NKJV
And as he was now going down, his servants met him and told him, saying, "Your son lives!"

9. What helped this man fully believe it was a miracle?

John 4:52 NKJV
Then he inquired of them the hour when he got better. And they said to him, "Yesterday at the seventh hour the fever left him."

10. What had Jesus said to the nobleman?

John 4:53 NKJV
So, the Father knew that it was at the same hour in which Jesus said to him, "Your son lives." And he himself believed, and his whole household.

11. What was the second miracle in Galilee?

John 4:54 NKJV
This again is the second sign Jesus did when He had come out of Judea into Galilee.

Answers:
1. A prophet will not be accepted in his hometown.
2. Because they had seen all the things he did in Jerusalem at the feast.
3. Because the nobleman remembered Jesus turned the water into wine.
4. The nobleman was pleading with Jesus because his son was sick unto death.
5. They are given to make believers (John 10:25-27,37,38)
6. The son was sick unto death.
7. Jesus's spoken word healed the son.
8. All is well, your son lives.
9. What time was he healed? Just knowing the moment Jesus spoke, was the time the son's health improved.
10. This got rid of any unbelief in the nobleman's heart, and he was able to testify of the power of God on Jesus.
11. The healing of the nobleman's son.

Outline:
- Your close family members may not accept your spiritual gifts and maturity.
- Seeing Jesus emotionally and physically heal others increases our belief.
- A miracle will give each of us a moment to choose to believe. To believe in the words and works of Jesus is intentional shifting from unbelief to belief.
- Don't wait until you are desperate to come to Jesus. But if you are desperate, come and ask for what you need.
- Hearing the Word of Jesus in my heart through reading and speaking the Word over my life will heal me emotionally.

Things to Ponder:
1. Who persecutes or mocks you for following Jesus closely? Forgive them.

2. Do you believe that Jesus will heal others, but not you?

3. How do you speak to yourself? Do you speak words of life or death over yourself?

Challenge: Anxiety/fear is a sign of unbelief. Settle yourself at the feet of Jesus until you hear His Words and then you will find the rest He has promised. This internal stillness requires practice it won't take long, and this quiet resting heart will be easy to find.

Write a prayer and ask the Lord to give you a quiet heart. Psalm 46:10

JOHN 5

Bethesda is the House of Mercy

He said to him, "Do you want to be made well?" John 5:6

Day 17

1. A. What had just happened?

   B. Then where did Jesus go?

John 5:1 NKJV
After this there was a feast of the Jews, and Jesus went up to Jerusalem.

2. A. Where was the pool?

   B. What was it called?

John 5:2 NKJV
Now there is in Jerusalem by the Sheep Gate a pool, which is called in Hebrew, Bethesda, having five porches.

3. A. Who lay around the porches?

B. Why would they lay by the pool all day?

John 5:3 NKJV
In these lay a great multitude of sick people, blind, lame, paralyzed, waiting for the moving of the water.

4. Why did people think this pool was so important?

John 5:4 NKJV For an angel went down at a certain time into the pool and stirred up the water; then whoever stepped in first, after the stirring of the water, was made well of whatever disease he had.

5. How long had the man been sick?

John 5:5 NKJV
Now a certain man was there who had an infirmity thirty-eight years.

6. A. Who initiated the conversation?

   B. What did Jesus ask the man?

John 5:6 NKJV
When Jesus saw him lying there, and knew that he already had been in that condition a long time, He said to him, "Do you want to be made well?"

7. How did the man answer?

John 5:7 NKJV
The sick man answered Him, "Sir, I have no man to put me into the pool when the water is stirred up; but while I am coming, another steps down before me."

8. What did Jesus say to him?

John 5:8 NKJV
Jesus said to him, "Rise, take up your bed and walk."

ANSWERS:
1. A. Feast of Jews had just happened. B. Then they went to Jerusalem.
2. A. The pool was by the sheep gate. B. It was called Bethesda which means house of mercy.
3. A. Impotent folk-weak, sick, helpless, blind, halt (lame), and withered (shrunk or paralyzed) people laid around the pool. B. They were waiting for the water to move.
4. A. An angel would go down at a certain time and trouble the water. When this happened the first person who stepped in was healed.
5. The man by the pool had been sick 38 years
6. A. Jesus initiated the conversation. B. Do you want to be made whole?
7. Sir, I have no one, when the water is troubled, to help me: somebody always gets ahead of me.
8. Get up, take your bed, and walk.

Outline:
- This hopeless man kept doing the same thing.
- The pool of Bethesda was a place in Jerusalem.
- An angel stirred the pool and the first one in was healed.
- The invalid man was perpetually waiting. He was trying to be first after the angel stirred the water. But was helpless to get there on his own.
- The sick man most likely felt hopeless, discouraged, and no way for future change.
- Do you want to be made well? It is important for us to desire to be well and not comfortable being sick.
- Jesus is the answer.

Things to Ponder:
3. Count how many helpless thoughts you have today?

4. Have you ever had an encounter with Jesus that changed your life?

5. Do you want to let go of the past and move forward towards health and wholeness?

Challenge: Practice taking defeating thoughts captive and exchange them for healthy strong thoughts. Write 2 Corinthians 10:4-5. Now practice renouncing thoughts you don't want to think and replacing them with new thoughts.

Write out a prayer and ask Jesus to show you any area of helplessness and pray for mercy?

Angie Meadows

Day 18

Jesus can make the sick whole.

"See, you have been made well. Sin no more, lest a worse thing come upon you." John 5:14

1. A. How soon was the man made whole?

   B. What day of the week was it?

John 5:9 NKJV
And immediately the man was made well, took up his bed, and walked. And that day was the Sabbath.

2. What did the Jews say to the cured man?

John 5:10 NKJV
The Jews therefore said to him who was cured, "It is the Sabbath; it is not lawful for you to carry your bed."

3. What did the healed man answer?

John 5:11 NKJV
He answered them, "He who made me well said to me, 'Take up your bed and walk.'"

4. What did the Jews ask him next?

John 5:12 NKJV
Then they asked him, "Who is the Man who said to you, 'Take up your bed and walk'?"

5. Did the healed man know who healed him?

John 5:13 NKJV
But the one who was healed did not know who it was, for Jesus had withdrawn, a multitude being in that place.

6. Later when Jesus found the healed man in the temple what warning does He give him?

John 5:14 NKJV
Afterward Jesus found him in the temple, and said to him, "See, you have been made well. Sin no more, lest a worse thing come upon you."

7. Do you think this man knew that the Jews wanted to harm Jesus?

John 5:15 NKJV
The man departed and told the Jews that it was Jesus who had made him well.

8. A. What was the reaction of the Jews?

   B. What was their main reason for the persecution?

John 5:16 NKJV
For this reason, the Jews persecuted Jesus, and sought to kill Him, because He had done these things on the Sabbath.

9. Did Jesus imply that His Father works on the Sabbath?

John 5:17 NKJV
But Jesus answered them, "My Father has been working until now, and I have been working."

10. For what greater reason did they seek to kill Jesus?

John 5:18 NKJV
Therefore, the Jews sought all the more to kill Him, because He not only broke the Sabbath, but also said that God was His Father, making Himself equal with God.

11. A. What relationship is Jesus to God?

    B. What can He do by Himself?

    C. What things does Jesus do?

*Later, we will explore the unity of the Father and Son.
John 5:19 NKJV
Then Jesus answered and said to them, "Most assuredly, I say to you, the Son can do nothing of Himself, but what He sees the Father do; for whatever He does, the Son also does in like manner.

Answers:
1. A. Immediately the man was made whole. B. It was the Sabbath day.
2. It is the Sabbath day: you are not allowed to carry your bed.
3. The one who healed me, told me to take up my bed and walk.
4. What man said that to you?
5. No, the healed man did not know who healed him.
6. Sin no more, so something worse don't happen.
7. We don't know.
8. A. They persecuted Jesus and sought to kill Him. B. They persecuted Jesus for healing on the Sabbath Day.
9. Yes, the Father works on the Sabbath.
10. He said God was His Father, making Himself equal with God.
11. A. Jesus is the Son of God. B. Jesus says He does nothing by Himself. C. Jesus does those things He sees the Father do.

Outline:
- Jesus did what was considered work on the Sabbath. He would heal on the Sabbath, and He commanded this man to pick up his bed and walk on the Sabbath.
- Jesus was more concerned about the man than about religious traditions.
- Mark 2:27-28 The Sabbath was made for mankind, not man for the Sabbath. And the Son of Man (Jesus) is Lord of the Sabbath.

- When others don't understand, they may try to entrap you and steal the joy the Lord has given you.
- When we find freedom in an area of life, we will lose it, if we return to toxic patterns.
- The Jews persecuted Jesus for His claim of oneness with the Father.

Things to Ponder:

1. Is there instructions Jesus has given you that you are reluctant to follow?

2. When you find an area of freedom in your life, do you set up boundaries and accountability, so you won't slide backwards?

3. How do you feel when others don't seem to understand you?

Challenge: Visualize a chronic situation that you can't change and release it to God. *Psalm 18:10 The name of the Lord is a strong tower...* can you visualize yourself on top of a high tower and push everything off the edge that is hindering you and causing you to be stuck in a negative emotion.

Write a prayer and ask God for deliverance from a long-term affliction (physical, emotional, financial, relationship, or spiritual).

Day 19

Belief is passing from Death unto Life.

I say to you, he who hears My word and believes in Him who sent Me has everlasting life, John 5:24

3. Why does God show Jesus all things that He does?

John 5:20 NKJV
For the Father loves the Son and shows Him all things that He Himself does; and He will show Him greater works than these, that you may marvel.

    4. A. Can the Father raise the dead?

    B. Does the Son have authority to resurrect who He wants?

John 5:21 NKJV
For as the Father raises the dead and gives life to them, even so the Son gives life to whom He will.

    5. Who will be the one that will judge?

John 5:22 NKJV
For the Father judges no one, but has committed all judgment to the Son,

    6. A. How should we honor Jesus?

    B. If we do not honor Jesus, can we honor the Father?

John 5:23 NKJV
that all should honor the Son just as they honor the Father. He who does not honor the Son does not honor the Father who sent Him.

    7. How can we come out of condemnation and have everlasting life?

John 5:24 NKJV
"Most assuredly, I say to you, he who hears My word and believes in Him who sent Me has everlasting life, and shall not come into judgment, but has passed from death into life.

    8.A. What dead is Jesus talking about?

    B. If we hear His voice, will we remain spiritually dead?

John 5:25 NKJV
Most assuredly, I say to you, the hour is coming, and now is, when the dead will hear the voice of the Son of God; and those who hear will live.

    9. What is Jesus's claim here?

John 5:26 NKJV
For as the Father has life in Himself, so He has granted the Son to have life in Himself,

    10. Again, it says God has given Jesus what?

John 5:27 NKJV
and has given Him authority to execute judgment also because He is the Son of Man.

    11. Who else other than the spiritually dead will hear Christ's voice?

John 5:28 NKJV
Do not marvel at this; for the hour is coming in which all who are in the graves will hear His voice...

12. When Jesus calls the physically dead from the graves what will happen to them?

John 5:29 NKJV
...and shall come forth-they that have done good, to the resurrection of life, and they that have done evil, to the resurrection of damnation.

Answers:
1. The Father shows Jesus all things He does because He loves the Son.
2. A. Yes, the Father can raise the dead. B. Yes, the Son has resurrection power.
3. Jesus has been given authority to judge.
4. A. When we want to honor Jesus, we honor the Father. B. We cannot honor one without the other.
5. There is no condemnation in Christ Jesus, so we must hear Christ's Word and believe on Him (God, the Father) that sent Him.
6. A. Jesus is speaking about the spiritually dead. B. We cannot remain dead after we have heard His spirit speak to us.
7. Jesus has life within Himself like the Father does.
8. Jesus has the authority to execute judgment.
9. Even the physically dead can hear the voice of Jesus.
10. When the physically dead are called from the graves, the good will have resurrection of life. The evil will have resurrection unto damnation.

Outline:
- The Father loves the Son, Jesus.
- Jesus has the authority to judge and resurrect.
- Self-condemnation is the law and places us under judgment of the Old Testament.
- Grace and mercy are the blessing of the New Testament and is a finished work of Christ to reconcile us to Him.
- Honoring Jesus=honoring the Father.
- Belief=everlasting life=no judgment
- Belief is passing from death into life.
- We need a physical and spiritual resurrection.

Things to Ponder:
1. If I could make a scale for my belief from 1-10, ten being the highest belief possible, what score would I give myself?

2. Anxiety is a signal of my unbelief. How much anxiety do I experience? Rate your anxiety from 1-10. Ten being extreme anxiety.

3. If I am in self-condemnation, am I abiding in life or death?

Challenge: Practice asking God a question and listening for the answer. How will I know who has a spirit of slumber? Romans 11:8

Write a prayer and ask God to awaken you from any spiritual slumber and open your ears that you may hear the voice of Jesus?
*Complaining is the language of a spiritually sluggish believer.

Book of John

Day 20

Prophets bear witness of the truth.

...because I do not seek My own will...John 5:30

1. A. Is Jesus claiming to do this on His own accord?

   B. Why is His judgment just or correct?

John 5:30 NKJV
I can of Myself do nothing. As I hear, I judge; and My judgment is righteous, because I do not seek My own will but the will of the Father who sent Me.

2. If Jesus witnessed of Himself would His witness be true?

John 5:31 NKJV
"If I bear witness of Myself, my witness is not true.

3. Is there another witness?

John 5:32 NKJV
There is another who bears witness of Me, and I know that the witness which He witnesses of Me is true.

4. Who bore witness of Jesus as the Messiah?

John 5:33 NKJV
You have sent to John, and he has borne witness to the truth.

5. Is the only testimony from a man?

John 5:34 NKJV
Yet I do not receive testimony from man, but I say these things that you may be saved.

6. Who was described as a burning and shining light?

John 5:35 NKJV
He was the burning and shining lamp, and you were willing for a time to rejoice in his light.

7. Who is the greater witness over John?

John 5:36 NKJV
But I have a greater witness than John's; for the works which the Father has given Me to finish-the very works that I do-bear witness of Me, that the Father has sent Me.

8. Had the Jews heard the voice of God or seen His shape?

John 5:37 NKJV
And the Father Himself, who sent Me, has testified of Me. You have neither heard His voice at any time, nor seen His form.

9. How does Jesus know that God's Word does not abide in these men?

John 5:38 NKJV
But you do not have His word abiding in you, because whom He sent, Him you do not believe.

Answers:
1. No, He is claiming unity with the Father. He does not seek His own will, but the will of the Father.
2. No, by law truth was established with a witness of two or more.
3. Yes, there is another witness.
4. John the Baptist bore witness of Jesus.
5. No, His testimony is not just from man.
6. John the Baptist was described as the burning and shining light.
7. The works that God gave Jesus to do are an even greater witness than John.
8. No, the Jews had not heard His voice or seen His form.
9. God's Word does not abide in men who do not believe in Christ.

Book of John

Outline:
- When we are full of Christ, we are full of life and light.
- Fullness in Christ is oneness with the Father.
- We become living witnesses to the work the Lord is doing in us.
- John the Baptist is called the burning and shining light.
- The Word cannot abide in you if you are in unbelief. It will leak right out.

Things to Ponder:
1. How much do you abide in unbelief: grieving, anger, bitterness, unforgiveness, self-pity, depression, lust, greed...?

2. What would it look like to intentionally abide in belief: life, hope, joy, peace, love, self-control, faithfulness...?

3. What would it feel like if the Lord called you His burning and shining light?

Challenge: Practice walking in peace and not letting anyone steal it from you. What is Jesus's instruction as to how you are to treat someone who steals your peace? Matthew 10:14

Write a prayer and ask God to make you aware of when you are agreeing with death and not abiding in life.

Book of John

Day 21

Moses wrote about Jesus.

...there is one who accuses you–Moses, in whom you trust.
John 5:44

1. How did the Jews search for eternal life?

John 5:39 NKJV
You search the Scriptures, for in them you think you have eternal life; and these are they which testify of Me.

2. How could these Jews have life?

John 5:40 NKJV
But you are not willing to come to Me that you may have life.

3. Does Jesus have the approval/honor of men?

John 5:41 NKJV
"I do not receive honor from men.

4. Those who persecute Jesus do not have what?

John 5:42 NKJV
But I know you, that you do not have the love of God in you.

5. A. When Jesus came in His Father's name did the Jews receive Him?

B. Who will the Jews receive in the future?

John 5:43 NKJV
I have come in My Father's name, and you do not receive Me; if another comes in his own name, him you will receive.

6. What is the reason these Jews cannot believe?

John 5:44 NKJV
How can you believe, who receive honor from one another, and do not seek the honor that comes from the only God?

7. Who will accuse these men?

John 5:45 NKJV
Do not think that I shall accuse you to the Father; there is one who accuses you-Moses, in whom you trust.

8. How will Moses accuse them?

John 5:46 NKJV
For if you believed Moses, you would believe Me; for he wrote about Me.

9. A. Do these men really believe Moses' writings?

    B. How can you tell?

*The Jews trusted in their laws and religion. They did not have a relationship with the Father.
John 5:47 NKJV
But if you do not believe his writings, how will you believe My words?"

Answers:
1. The Jews searched for eternal life by searching the Scriptures.
2. Life comes to you when you come to Jesus.
3. Jesus has approval from the Father and does not need the approval of men.
4. Those who persecute Jesus do not have the love of God.

5. A. No, the Jews did not receive Jesus. B. One day they will receive one who comes in his own name.
6. These Jews cannot believe because they seek honor from one another and not from God.
7. Moses will accuse these men through the written Word.
8. It will be the words of Moses that they trust in that will accuse them because the words of Moses speak of Jesus.
9. A. No, they didn't believe. B. We know they didn't because they didn't believe Jesus's words either.

Outline:
- Searching the Scripture is in vain if we do not believe.
- Coming to Jesus and believing upon Him brings life.
- Those who want the honor of men, do not receive the honor of God.
- Persecutors have no love for God, the Father, in them.

Things to Ponder:
1. How can I recognize my need to receive gratitude or honor from people?

2. How do I act if I am not appreciated or noticed by others?

3. Can I develop compassion in the face of persecution by understanding that people who persecute others are abiding in unbelief and death and need boundaries and compassion?

Challenge: Choose one word and look up a few verses and research their meanings in a Bible commentary.
Resting
Healings
Glory
Persecution
Light
Life
Blessing

Write a prayer and ask God to help you love Him more. Ask Him for a deeper awareness of His presence.

JOHN 6

Jesus is there in time of need.

Gather up the fragments that remain that nothing be lost.
John 6:12

Day 22

2. Where did Jesus go next?

John 6:1 NKJV
After these things Jesus went over the Sea of Galilee, which is the Sea of Tiberias.

3. Why did the multitude follow Jesus?

John 6:2 NKJV
Then a great multitude followed Him, because they saw His signs which He performed on those who were diseased.

4. So, what did Jesus do?

John 6:3 NKJV
And Jesus went up on the mountain, and there He sat with His disciples.

5. What time of year was close?

John 6:4 NKJV
Now the Passover, a feast of the Jews, was near.

6. What did Jesus ask Phillip?

John 6:5 NKJV
Then Jesus lifted His eyes, and seeing a great multitude coming toward Him, He said to Philip, "Where shall we buy bread, that these may eat?"

7. Why did He ask Phillip this question?

John 6:6 NKJV
But this He said to test him, for He Himself knew what He would do.

8. Did Phillip think that they could feed the great company of people following Jesus?

John 6:7 NKJV
Philip answered Him, "Two hundred denarii worth of bread is not sufficient for them, that every one of them may have a little."

9. Who is speaking next?

John 6:8 NKJV
One of His disciples, Andrew, Simon Peter's brother, said to Him,

10. A. What did Andrew find?

B. What was Andrew's question?

John 6:9 NKJV
"There is a lad here who has five barley loaves and two small fish, but what are they among so many?"

11. A. What did Jesus tell them to do?

B. How many people were there?

John 6:10 NKJV
Then Jesus said, "Make the people sit down." Now there was much grass in the place. So, the men sat down, in number about five thousand.

12. A. What do you think Jesus' emphasis was on the thanksgiving to God or the food?

   B. What did the disciples do?

John 6:11 NKJV
And Jesus took the loaves, and when He had given thanks, He distributed them to the disciples, and the disciples to those sitting down; and likewise of the fish, as much as they wanted.

13. Can you find a principle here?

John 6:12 NKJV
So, when they were filled, He said to His disciples, "Gather up the fragments that remain, so that nothing is lost."

14. How much was left?

John 6:13 NKJV
Therefore, they gathered them up, and filled twelve baskets with the fragments of the five barley loaves which were left over by those who had eaten.

Answers:
1. Jesus went over the Sea to Galilee.
2. The multitude followed because of the miracles.
3. Jesus went up into the mountains and sat with His disciples.
4. The Passover was near.
5. Where will we buy bread, so we can feed these people?
6. Jesus asked Philip to test Him.
7. No, Phillip thought it was impossible.
8. Andrew is speaking, He is Simon Peter's brother.
9. A. Andrew found five barley loaves and two small fishes. B. But what are they among so many?
10. A. Jesus said have the people to sit down.
B. There were 5,000 people there to feed.
11. A. Jesus's emphasis was on thanksgiving to God. B. The disciples distributed the food.

12. **Do not be wasteful.** Gather up the fragments that remain that nothing be lost.
13. There were 12 baskets left over.

Outline:
- They are by the Sea of Galilee also known as Tiberias.
- There was a great multitude that followed Jesus because of the miracles He had done.
- Jesus was in the Mountains with His disciples when He saw the crowd coming.
- The time of the year was Passover.
- Jesus tested Philip and asked Him how they would feed the multitude. Philip was in the earthly realm and reasoned it was impossible.
- Andrew noted the meager provisions of 5 loaves and 2 fishes.
- Jesus gave the command for the multitude to "sit down".
- Jesus gave thanks for the food. Jesus already knew what He would do.
- At the end, Jesus commanded the disciples to gather up the fragments. There were twelve baskets of leftovers. This would be enough for a basket for each disciple.

Things to Ponder:
1. Is there an impossibility in your life where you only see limitations?

2. Do you have a lack of provisions in your life that you could ask Jesus to multiply?

3. When we share what we have with a thankful heart, we always have an abundance. What do you feel like God is calling you to share?

What do you have in storage that you no longer use that another person may need?

Challenge: If someone takes something of yours, give them the best of something else. Practice sharing in your own life. Matthew 5:41; Luke 6:29.

Bonus Challenge: We balance this with the verses that say do not cast your pearls before swine. Matthew 7:6 And the principle of not giving to someone who is a poor steward and will destroy everything you give them and be entitled and think everything of yours is theirs. 1 Peter 4:10

With the <u>first challenge</u> the principle is to give and share with others taking from you so you will not carry an offense against them. The <u>second challenge</u> is stewardship. It directs us to make wise decisions with those things that are within our control.

Write a prayer and ask God to give you a pure heart.

Day 23

Jesus Walks on the Storms of Life

It is I; be not afraid. John 6:20

1. Now what did the people think of Jesus?

John 6:14 NKJV
Then those men, when they had seen the sign that Jesus did, said, "This is truly the Prophet who is to come into the world."

2. When Jesus was about to be exalted what did He do?

John 6:15 NKJV
Therefore, when Jesus perceived that they were about to come and take Him by force to make Him king, He departed again to the mountain by Himself alone.

3. Where did His disciples go?

John 6:16 NKJV
Now when evening came, His disciples went down to the sea,

4. A. What did they do when they got to the sea?

   B. What time of day was it?

John 6:17 NKJV
got into the boat and went over the sea toward Capernaum. And it was already dark, and Jesus had not come to them.

5. Why was the sea choppy and full of waves?

John 6:18 NKJV
Then the sea arose because a great wind was blowing.

6. A. When they had rowed about five and twenty or thirty furlongs about 4 miles what did they see?

   B. How did they feel?

John 6:19 NKJV
So, when they had rowed about three or four miles, they saw Jesus walking on the sea and drawing near the boat; and they were afraid.

7. A. Did Jesus perceive their fear?

   B. With what words did He comfort them?

John 6:20 NKJV
But He said to them, "It is I; do not be afraid."

8. A. When the disciples realized it was Jesus what did they do?

   B. Then what miracle happened?

John 6:21 NKJV
Then they willingly received Him into the boat, and immediately the boat was at the land where they were going.

Answers:
1. The people said this is the prophet (Messiah) that was to come.
2. He went to the mountain alone.
3. The disciples went to the sea.
4. A. They entered a boat and went over the sea toward Capernaum. B. It was already dark, so late evening or nighttime.
5. The sea arose because of a great wind.
6. A. They saw Jesus walking on the water. B. The disciples were afraid.
7. A. Yes, He did. He announced Himself and told them not to be afraid. B. It's me!

8. A. The disciples received Him into the boat. B. They were immediately at their destination.

Outline:
- The people saw Jesus as the prophet that should come.
- The people wanted to force their way of thinking onto Jesus and make Him king of the Jews. They saw what He could do for them by multiplying the food.
- The disciples were in the boat and the storm arose.
- Jesus came to them walking on the water.
- As soon as they recognized and received Jesus, the storm was calm.
- Jesus assured them that it was Him and told them to not be afraid.
- Immediately the storm ceased when Jesus entered the disciples boat.

Things to Ponder:
1. Are there any struggles that are relentless that you think if you just prayed harder, God would fix it?

2. Reshape the next storm in your life by quoting, "It is I; be not afraid." John 6:20 Peace comes as we see Jesus in every storm.

3 Jesus is the destination. As soon as they received Jesus into the boat, the storm not only ceased, but they were immediately at their destination. Invite Jesus into your circumstance and obey the command: "be not afraid."

Challenge: What in your life looks evil (like a bad storm) that you need to accept as if it is from the hand of God? Job 2:10

Bonus Challenge: Find a white handkerchief or cloth and wave a flag of surrender as a reminder to you of the things you cannot control. As you wave the flag, take a deep breath, and release the problem to the Lord.

Write a prayer and ask God for the grace to help you surrender everything that is causing you fear, anxiety, or stress.

Angie Meadows

Day 24

Let miracles lead to belief.

Labor... for the meat which endures unto everlasting life.
John 6:27

1. Why were the people at Capernaum puzzled?

John 6:22 NKJV
On the following day, when the people who were standing on the other side of the sea saw that there was no other boat there, except that one which His disciples had entered, and that Jesus had not entered the boat with His disciples, but His disciples had gone away alone-

2. What were the people doing the next day?

John 6:23 NKJV
however, other boats came from Tiberias, near the place where they ate bread after the Lord had given thanks-

3. A. When they didn't find Him what did they do?

   B. Why would they have thought to go to Capernaum?

John 6:24 NKJV
when the people therefore saw that Jesus was not there, nor His disciples, they also got into boats and came to Capernaum, seeking Jesus.

4. When they found Him in Capernaum what did they ask Him?

John 6:25 NKJV

And when they found Him on the other side of the sea, they said to Him, "Rabbi, when did You come here?"

5. Why were they seeking Jesus?

John 6:26 NKJV
Jesus answered them and said, "Most assuredly, I say to you, you seek Me, not because you saw the signs, but because you ate of the loaves and were filled.

6. What was Jesus's instructions?

John 6:27 NKJV
Do not labor for the food which perishes, but for the food which endures to everlasting life, which the Son of Man will give you, because God the Father has set His seal on Him."

7. What question did the people ask?

John 6:28 NKJV
Then they said to Him, "What shall we do, that we may work the works of God?"

8. What is the work of God?

John 6:29 NKJV
Jesus answered and said to them, "This is the work of God, that you believe in Him whom He sent."

9. What did the people seek?

John 6:30 NKJV
Therefore, they said to Him, "What sign will You perform then, that we may see it and believe You? What work will You do?

Answers:
1. The disciples came over the sea alone and there was no other boat present and yet Jesus was with them.
2. The people were looking for Jesus.
3. They took a ship to Capernaum to seek Jesus. B. Because they knew Jesus would be with His disciples and they had seen the disciples leave.
4. Rabbi, how did You get here?

5. They had eaten the loaves of bread and were filled.
6. Labor not for meat that will perish, but for food that last unto eternal life.
7. "What shall we do, that we may work the works of God?"
8. The work we are to do is to believe on Jesus whom God has sent.
9. The people sought a sign or work.

Outline:
- The people sought Jesus by following the disciples.
- The people couldn't figure out how Jesus got across the sea when He didn't leave in the boat with the disciples.
- They followed Jesus not for miracles to lead to belief but, because they were carnal with a fleshly appetite.
- The work of God is for us to believe.
- But the people sought for a sign, not for the purpose of believing.

Things to Ponder:
1 Can you recognize your motive for seeking? Is it to believe on the one the Father sent?

2 Rehearse John 6:29 and tell me again what the work of God is for you?

3 Do you praise God for unanswered prayers?

Challenge: Unbelief is exhibited by fear, worry, fretfulness, and anxiety. Practice moving all anxiety by leaning not to your own understanding, but simply acknowledging the sovereignty of God. What are the instructions in Proverbs 3:6?

Write a prayer and ask God to help you exercise and build your trust muscle by renouncing the anxiety in your life and learning to rehearse a promise.

If you don't know a promise rehearse this one until it rolls automatically from your tongue when you face darkness: *Nay, in all these things we are more than <u>conquerors</u> through Him that loved us. Romans 8:37*

Angie Meadows

Day 25

Jesus is the Bread of Life

...him that comes to me I will in no wise cast out. John 6:37

1. What kind of sign are they asking for?

John 6:31 NKJV
Our Fathers ate the manna in the desert; as it is written, 'He gave them bread from heaven to eat.'"

2. What was Jesus's answer about the type of bread they were asking for?

John 6:32 NKJV
Then Jesus said to them, "Most assuredly, I say to you, Moses did not give you the bread from heaven, but My Father gives you the true bread from heaven.

3. Who is the true bread of God and what will He do?

John 6:33 NKJV
For the bread of God is He who comes down from heaven and gives life to the world."

4. Did the people understand that they needed spiritual bread?

John 6:34 NKJV
Then they said to Him, "Lord, give us this bread always."

5. A. Who is the Bread of Life?

B. Jesus says if we come to Him, we will never what?

C. If we believe on Him, we will never what?

John 6:35 NKJV
And Jesus said to them, "I am the bread of life. He who comes to Me shall never hunger, and he who believes in Me shall never thirst.

6. What does Jesus say about them?

John 6:36 NKJV
But I said to you that you have seen Me and yet do not believe.

7. A. What are we to do?

B. If we come to Jesus with our whole heart will He cast us out?

John 6:37 NKJV
All that the Father gives Me will come to Me, and the one who comes to Me I will by no means cast out.

8. What example is He giving us for our lives?

John 6:38 NKJV
For I have come down from heaven, not to do My own will, but the will of Him who sent Me.

9. Can we trust Jesus to hold onto us?

John 6:39 NKJV
This is the will of the Father who sent Me, that of all He has given Me I should lose nothing but should raise it up at the last day.

10. What's the will of God?

John 6:40 NKJV
And this is the will of Him who sent Me, that everyone who sees the Son and believes in Him may have everlasting life; and I will raise him up at the last day."

11.   A. What was the Jews reaction?

     B. What were they murmuring about?

*Murmuring is usually a sign of unbelief.
John 6:41 NKJV
The Jews then complained about Him, because He said, "I am the bread which came down from heaven."

Answers:
1. The people are asking for bread (manna) coming from heaven.
2. Moses didn't give you the bread from heaven (just temporal bread), but it is my Father who gives you the true bread.
3. The true bread is Jesus, and He gives <u>life</u> unto the world.
4. No, they didn't understand but they were asking for it.
5. A. Jesus is the bread of life. B. If we come, we will never be hungry. C. You will never thirst again.
6. You have seen Me and still don't believe.
7. A. We are to come. B. No, the Lord will never cast us out when we come.
8. Don't walk in self-will, but in the will of the Father.
9. Yes, we can trust Jesus to hold us.
10. The promise is that everyone who believes on Jesus will have everlasting life and resurrection.
11. The Jews reaction was murmuring. B. The people were complaining because Jesus said, I am the bread from heaven.

Outline:
1. Bread of heaven from Moses was sustaining.
2. Jesus is the true bread from heaven.
3. "I am the bread of life."
4. Jesus says, believe on Me.
5. Jesus says anyone who comes to Me I will not cast out.
6. Jesus does the will of the Father.
7. Jesus won't lose any of us but will raise us up in the last day to everlasting life.
8. Belief leads to everlasting life.

Things to Ponder:
1. Read Jeremiah 15:16 and tell me what blessing we receive when we eat the bread of true life?

2. Unbelief keeps me temporal focused. Am I hungry and thirsty enough to come to Jesus and eat the bread of life?

3. What am I working for that will last throughout all eternity?

Challenge: Name three circumstances in your life that has caused you suffering. Reframe your trials and intentionally practice joy. Counting your trials joy is spiritual maturity skill rooted in belief. Read James 1:2-4 and rehearse bits of it three times today.

Write a prayer and ask God to give you His joy that you may have strength. Nehemiah 8:10

Day 26

Murmuring=Unbelief

Do not murmur among yourselves. John 6:43

1. What are they doing?

John 6:42 NKJV
And they said, "Is not this Jesus, the son of Joseph, whose Father and mother we know? How is it then that He says, 'I have come down from heaven'?"

2. A. Did Jesus perceive their murmurings?

   B. What did Jesus say to them?

John 6:43 NKJV
Jesus therefore answered and said to them, "Do not murmur among yourselves.

3. A. If we are in murmuring and unbelief what do we need to pray for?

   B. What reward will we receive in the last day?

John 6:44 NKJV
No one can come to Me unless the Father who sent Me draws him; and I will raise him up at the last day.

4. What is our responsibility so God will draw us unto Himself?

John 6:45 NKJV

It is written in the prophets, 'And they shall all be taught by God.' Therefore, everyone who has heard and learned from the Father comes to Me.

5. Who can see the Father?

John 6:46 NKJV
Not that anyone has seen the Father, except He who is from God; He has seen the Father.

6. What reward will we receive with faithful and continual belief?

John 6:47 NKJV
Most assuredly, I say to you, he who believes in Me has everlasting life.

7. A. Jesus said, "I am" what?

   B. Who is our daily bread?

John 6:48 NKJV
I am the bread of life.

8. Can we eat meat that won't endure unto everlasting life?

John 6:49 NKJV
Your Fathers ate the manna in the wilderness and are dead.

9. If we eat of the bread of Christ, will we die?

John 6:50 NKJV
This is the bread which comes down from heaven, that one may <u>eat of it and not die.</u>

10. A. What is so special about the Bread from Christ?

    B. What does it mean to eat of the bread of Christ?

John 6:51 NKJV
I am the living bread which came down from heaven. If anyone eats of this bread, he will live forever; and the bread that I shall give is My flesh, which I shall give for the life of the world."

Answers:
1. The people are making excuses as to why they can't believe in Jesus.
2. A. Yes, Jesus knew all things.
B. Jesus commands us to murmur not.
3. A. We need to pray that the Father who sent Jesus will draw us unto Him.
B. The reward is resurrection unto life.
4. Our responsibility is to hear and learn.
5. We can see the Father through Jesus.
6. Belief leads to everlasting life.
7. A. I am the Bread of Life. B. Jesus is our daily bread.
8. Yes, there is an earthly manna.
9. Physically yes, we will die, but spiritually no.
10. A. Christ is the "living bread". B. Eating the Bread is to come, believe, hear, learn, and do the will of the Father, and to follow Christ.

Outline:
- Unbelievers murmur.
- Unbelieving believers speak doubt.
- The unbelievers will rationalize circumstances to outweigh the miracles they see.
- No man has the power to come to Christ on His own.
- Those that hear and learn will come.
- Belief is everlasting life.
- "I am" the bread of life.
- Eat of Christ and you will not die.
- Bread of Jesus is living bread.
- Jesus gave His flesh for the life of the world.

Things to Ponder:
1. Listen to your thoughts today. Do you hear yourself rationalizing why you can't completely follow Jesus?

2. Do you mock other believers as radicals or Jesus freaks if they have experiences you don't understand?

Are you mocked for following Jesus?

3. Flesh cannot give flesh life. True worship will worship God in Spirit and in truth. John 4:24 Ask God to awaken your spirit and open your spiritual ears. Matthew 11:15

Challenge: My belief is directly connected to how much my spiritual ear is tuned to hear spiritual truth. Romans 10:17 It pleases God to save those who believe by the foolishness of preaching. 1 Corinthians 1:21

Write a prayer and ask the Lord to tune your ear to sound doctrine. If you struggle with confusion, I challenge you to study as much of the Word as you can handle. 2 Timothy 2:15

Day 27

Truth and Faith abide together.

...he who feeds on Me will live because of Me. John 6:57

1. What did the Jews lack in this verse?

John 6:52 NKJV
The Jews therefore quarreled among themselves, saying, "How can this Man give us His flesh to eat?"

2. A. What does eating His flesh mean?

   B. What does drinking His blood mean?

John 6:53 NKJV
Then Jesus said to them, "Most assuredly, I say to you, unless you eat the flesh of the Son of Man and drink His blood, you have no life in you.

3. If we believe on Christ and accept His blood to wash away our sins what is the promise?

John 6:54 NKJV
Whoever eats My flesh and drinks My blood has eternal life, and I will raise him up at the last day.

4. A. His flesh is our what?

   B. His blood is our what?

Book of John

* We grow spiritually when we eat the life of the Word and drink deeply of forgiveness for others and ourselves.

John 6:55 NKJV
For My flesh is food indeed, and My blood is drink indeed.
*He commands us to spiritually **eat and drink** of <u>truth</u> through <u>faith</u> in Him.

5. What do you think oneness with Christ feels like?

John 6:56 NKJV
He who eats My flesh and drinks My blood abides in Me, and I in him.

6. When we are in Christ will we live for ourselves or Christ?

John 6:57 NKJV
As the living Father sent Me, and I live because of the Father, so he who feeds on Me will live because of Me.

7. Is the bread Christ is offering physical or spiritual bread?

John 6:58 NKJV
This is the bread which came down from heaven-not as your Fathers ate the manna and are dead. He who eats this bread will live forever."

8. Where did Jesus say these things?

John 6:59 NKJV
These things He said in the synagogue as He taught in Capernaum.

Answers:
1. The Jews lacked understanding.
2. A. Eating Jesus's flesh is believing on Him in faith. It means partaking of the benefits of Christ death. B. We must receive His atoning blood which washes away our sins.
3. The promise is everlasting life and resurrection at the last day.
4. Jesus's flesh is our food/meat. Jesus's blood is our drink. We grow by eating and drinking physically.
5. Oneness with Christ is peace. (John 14:27)
6. We will live for Christ.
7. Christ offers the spiritual bread from heaven.
8. Jesus was teaching in the synagogue in Capernaum.

Outline:
- Jews quarreled among themselves.
- Eat His flesh and drink His blood = life
- Jesus will raise us up in the last days.
- Jesus is the food from heaven and the water from the Rock. Jesus is the Rock.

Things to Ponder:
1. There are spiritual eyes that need to be enlightened. Unless we eat the Words of Christ in faith our eyes cannot see past our temporal circumstances. Eternal vision requires spiritual eyes. Pray to have your spiritual eyes enlightened. Ephesians 1:18

2. Pray for a vision for the future. Without a supernatural vision we will perish. Proverbs 29:18

3. When I am struggling to believe, pray for grace to have more faith. Ephesians 2:8

Challenge: Normally, I fight with myself more than I fight with anyone else. If I can be quiet before the Lord, I can hear where I am wrestling. The Lord commands me to be still. Find a second command in this verse? Psalm 46:10 What would it look like to be still (quiet internally)?

What would it look like to stop trying to be your own god?

Write a prayer and ask God to teach you how to be still before Him and to quiet your own heart.

Day 28

Unbelief carries Offenses.

Does this offend you? John 6:61

1. Was Jesus's teaching easy or hard to receive?

*Receiving the Lord's sayings requires faith.
John 6:60 NKJV
Therefore, many of His disciples, when they heard this, said, "This is a hard saying; who can understand it?"

2. A. Now who is murmuring?

   B. What did Jesus ask them?

John 6:61 NKJV
When Jesus knew in Himself that His disciples complained about this, He said to them, "Does this offend you?

3. What future event is He talking about that they are going to struggle with receiving unless they exercise their faith?

John 6:62 NKJV
What then if you should see the Son of Man ascend where He was before?

4. Can we understand the Bible in our flesh?

John 6:63 NKJV

Book of John

It is the Spirit who gives life; the flesh profits nothing. The words that I speak to you are spirit, and they are life.

5. A. Did Jesus know who believed and who didn't?

   B. Did He know He would be betrayed?

John 6:64 NKJV
But there are some of you who do not believe." For Jesus knew from the beginning who they were who did not believe, and who would betray Him.

6. Who needs to enable us to come to Christ?

John 6:65 NKJV
And He said, "Therefore I have said to you that no one can come to Me unless it has been granted to him by My Father."

7. Did this teaching a separate true and false believers?

John 6:66 NKJV
From that time many of His disciples went back and walked with Him no more.
*When the going gets tough, it will test our belief and bring out any unbelief in our hearts that needs repentance and correction.

8. A. Did the twelve leave Jesus?

   B. What did Jesus ask them?

John 6:67 NKJV
Then Jesus said to the twelve, "Do you also want to go away?"

9. What did Peter ask Jesus?

*Jesus has the Words of eternal life.
John 6:68 NKJV

But Simon Peter answered Him, "Lord, to whom shall we go? You have the words of eternal life.

10. What is Peter declaration?

John 6:69 NKJV
Also, we have come to believe and know that You are the Christ, the Son of the living God."

11. A. Who chose the twelve?

   B. Do all the twelve believe?

John 6:70 NKJV
Jesus answered them, "Did I not choose you, the twelve, and one of you is a devil?"

12. Which one is called the devil?

John 6:71 NKJV
He spoke of Judas Iscariot, the son of Simon, for it was he who would betray Him, being one of the twelve.

Answers:
1. Jesus's teaching was hard to receive.
2. A. The disciples are murmuring. B. Jesus asked if His words offended them?
3. Jesus is talking about His ascension.
4. No. The spirit must be quickened that it may hear the Words of life.
5. A. Yes, Jesus knew who believed and who didn't. B. Yes, betrayal by one who shared His own bread was prophecy. Psalm 41:9; Luke 22:47,48
6. God, the Father, must grant us access to Jesus.
7. Yes, Jesus's teaching divided those who believed from those who did not believe.
8. A. No, true disciples will never fall away. B. Will you all also go away?
9. Peter asked, Lord, to whom shall we go?
10. Peter declares that Jesus is the Christ, the Son of the Living God.
11. A. Jesus, chose the twelve. B. No, one is a devil and does not believe unto salvation.
12. Judas Iscariot, the betrayer that Satan enters, is called a devil.

Outline:
- Jesus's teaching was hard to receive.
- Murmuring is a sign of unbelief.
- God draws us to Him.
- Many shall fall away because of unbelief.
- Jesus has the Words of eternal life.
- Peter declares Jesus as the Messiah.
- A close friend can be a devil and will eventually expose themselves.

Things to Ponder:
1. Jesus did not shrink from His purpose when others didn't believe in Him. He knew what He believed. Is there an area of your life where you are double-minded (James 1:8) and don't know what you believe? *Doublemindedness causes instability.

2. What do you do if you lack wisdom? James 1:5.

3. Evaluate your speech today. Ask God to help you recognize when you murmur, grumble, or complain. This will help you identify areas of unbelief in your life.
*What we complain about identifies our areas of unbelief.

Challenge: Identify the areas of your life this last year where you were betrayed. This will be the area with the most confusion and the most emotional pain. Outline David's betrayal prayer in the Psalm 41:9-13

Write a prayer and ask God to double your love for Him. Write out Psalm 18:1. Now tell me who is your strength?

Book of John

John 7

Jesus secretly went.

...the Jews sought to kill Him. John 7:1

Day 29

1. A. Where did Jesus go next?

   B. Why did He leave Jerusalem?

John 7:1 NKJV
After these things Jesus walked in Galilee; for He did not want to walk in Judea, because the Jews sought to kill Him.

2. What feast was about to happen?

*It's in the fall; 7 months before Jesus' death.
John 7:2 NKJV
Now the Jews' Feast of Tabernacles was at hand.

3. What did His brethren want Jesus to do?

John 7:3 NKJV
His brothers therefore said to Him, "Depart from here and go into Judea, that Your disciples also may see the works that You are doing.

4. Jesus was traveling through the small villages and country sides, but they wanted Jesus to go to the city. Why?

John 7:4 NKJV
For no one does anything in secret while he himself seeks to be known openly. If You do these things, show Yourself to the world."

5. Did His brothers believe in Him as the Messiah?

John 7:5 NKJV
For even His brothers did not believe in Him.

6. What was Jesus' answer?

John 7:6 NKJV
Then Jesus said to them, "My time has not yet come, but your time is always ready.

7. A. Why did the world hate Jesus?

B. Does the world hate those that belong to it?

John 7:7 NKJV
The world cannot hate you, but it hates Me because I testify of it that its works are evil.

8. What did Jesus tell them to do?

John 7:8 NKJV
You go up to this feast. I am not yet going up to this feast, for My time has not yet fully come."

9. Where did He stay?

John 7:9 NKJV
When He had said these things to them, He remained in Galilee.

10. Did Jesus go openly to the feast?

John 7:10 NKJV
But when His brothers had gone up, then He also went up to the feast, not openly, but as it were in secret.

11. Who sought Him at the feast?

John 7:11 NKJV
Then the Jews sought Him at the feast, and said, "Where is He?"

Answers:
1. A. Jesus went to Galilee next. B. Jesus left Jerusalem because the Jews sought to kill Him.
2. It was the Jew's Feast of Tabernacles.
3. They wanted Jesus to go to Judea and show His works.
4. They wanted Him to travel to the city because they didn't want His work to be secret, but for His fame to increase.
5. No. They thought He was just a prophet.
6. My time has not yet come. He may have been referring to His time of suffering ahead or He may have had other things to do before going to the feast.
7. A. Jesus says their works are evil. B. No, the world does not hate their own.
8. Jesus told them to go to the feast (there was probably a caravan traveling).
9. Jesus stayed in Galilee.
10. No, Jesus went in secret.
11. The Jewish leaders sought Him at the feast.

Outline:
- The Jews seek to kill Jesus.
- The time of the year is the Feast of Tabernacles.
- Jesus's brethren wanted Him to go and do miracles and let His fame spread.
- Jesus knew it wasn't time to move forward in His ministry.
- The world's works are evil.
- Jesus goes to the feast in secret.
- Jewish leaders are looking for Him.

Things To Ponder:
1. Jesus knew He wasn't safe at the feast and at first went secretly because of the hostility of the Pharisees. Is there a place where you don't feel safe? If so, how could you position yourself to move in and out quickly with emotional detachment from the toxicity of a situation?

2. Is it time? Has your time come? Or is there waiting and maturing that needs to be done in your spirit before you move forward with your purpose in life.

Challenge: Name an area of your life where you need maturity. This can be identified by anything in your day that causes you irritation or robs your peace.

Write a prayer and ask God to help you monitor your speech and discover if you are pre-judging others without knowing all the facts.

Day 30

Intentional Obedience knows the Will of God!

If anyone wills to do His will... John 7:17

1. What things did they say when they were complaining?

John 7:12 NKJV
And there was much complaining among the people concerning Him. Some said, "He is good"; others said, "No, on the contrary, He deceives the people."

2. What was the potential snare that kept men from speaking openly of Him?

John 7:13 NKJV
However, no one spoke openly of Him for fear of the Jews.

3. Amid the feast what did Jesus do?

John 7:14 NKJV
Now about the middle of the feast Jesus went up into the temple and taught.

4. Why did the Jews marvel at His teachings?

John 7:15 NKJV
And the Jews marveled, saying, "How does this Man know letters, having never studied?"

5. Whose doctrine does Jesus teach?

John 7:16 NKJV
Jesus answered them and said, "My doctrine is not Mine, but His who sent Me.

6. What is our responsibility to do to understand true doctrine?

John 7:17 NKJV
If anyone wills to do His will, he shall know concerning the doctrine, whether it is from God or whether I speak on My own authority.

7. A. Jesus seeks to glorify who?

B. Who seeks his own glory?

John 7:18 NKJV
He who speaks from himself seeks his own glory; but He who seeks the glory of the One who sent Him is true, and no unrighteousness is in Him.

Answers:
1. He is a good man. Nay: but He deceives the people.
2. The fear of man (Jewish leaders) prevented people from speaking freely about Jesus.
3. Jesus went to the temple and taught.
4. Because He was not learned in letters and had never been trained.
5. Jesus teaches God's doctrine.
6. We just purpose to do the will of God.
7. A. Jesus seeks to glorify God, the Father. B. Those who speak of themselves seek their own glory.

Outline:
- The Jewish leaders sought Jesus.
- A difference of opinions causes murmuring and complaining.
- People had the fear of Jewish leaders.
- Jesus taught them at the feast.
- The Jews marveled at how an unlearned man could teach with such authority.
- Jesus teaches the doctrine of the Father.
- If you want to do God's will, then you will be able to discern it.
- Jesus seeks the Father's glory.

Things to Ponder:
1. Do you have a fear of man in any area of your life? Is there a boss, parent, or spouse that you appease and tiptoe around? If so, this behavior needs processed and talked about with strong supportive friends or a counselor.

2. Psalm 119:98 says the commandments make us wiser than our teachers. The purpose of reading and studying the Word of God is so we will know how to find the precepts, principles, statutes, and commandments in God's Word to guide our life.

3. 2 Timothy 2:15 describes to us the foundation of a person's life that never needs to be ashamed. It is in studying the Word of God that helps us divide error from truth. Pray and ask God to give you the desire to study his Word.

Challenge: Study is an active word. How will you discipline yourself to actively study his Word? What can you do if you get off track?

Write a prayer and ask God to give you the grace to be steadfastly devoted to Him in all your ways. Write out Psalm 51:10

Angie Meadows

Day 31

Judge Rightly

Do not judge according to appearance...John 7:24

1. A. The Jews trusted in the law of Moses. Yet, can anyone keep the law?

   B. Why did they want to kill Jesus?

John 7:19 NKJV
Did not Moses give you the law, yet none of you keeps the law? Why do you seek to kill Me?"

2. Now what is the accusation towards Jesus?

John 7:20 NKJV
The people answered and said, "You have a demon. Who is seeking to kill You?"

3. Do you know what work Jesus is referring? John 5:9,10,16

John 7:21 NKJV
Jesus answered and said to them, "I did one work, and you all marvel.

4. What does Jesus say they do on the Sabbath?

John 7:22 NKJV
Moses therefore gave you circumcision (not that it is from Moses, but from the Fathers), and you circumcise a man on the Sabbath.

5. Jesus is comparing what to healing on the Sabbath?

John 7:23 NKJV

If a man receives circumcision on the Sabbath, so that the law of Moses should not be broken, are you angry with Me because I made a man completely well on the Sabbath?

6. A. How does Jesus tell them not to judge?

   B. How are they to judge?

John 7:24 NKJV
Do not judge according to appearance, but judge with righteous judgment."

7. Did the people know they wanted to kill Jesus?

John 7:25 NKJV
Now some of them from Jerusalem said, "Is this not He whom they seek to kill?

8. A. What tone is Jesus using to speak?

   B. What is the question?

John 7:26 NKJV
But look! He speaks boldly, and they say nothing to Him. Do the rulers know indeed that this is truly the Christ?
*Jesus doesn't mind disputing with the rulers.

Answers:
1. A. No, no one can keep the law. B. They sought to kill Him for breaking the Law of Moses by doing work on the Sabbath day.
2. They accused Jesus of having a devil. They twisted His words. They denied that they were trying to kill Him.
3. Jesus is referring to healing on the Sabbath.
4. Jesus rationalizes that they break the law by circumcising on the Sabbath.
5. Jesus is comparing healing and circumcision.
6. A. Jesus tells them to not judge by appearance. B. They are to judge righteously.
7. Yes, the people referred to Jesus as the one the leaders wanted to kill.
8. A. Jesus is speaking boldly to them. B. Do the rulers know indeed that this is the very Christ?

Outline:
- The leaders thought sabbath healing was breaking the law of Moses and sought to kill Him.
- Then they pretended that He was crazy and that they weren't seeking to kill Him.
- Jesus challenges their thinking about the Sabbath. Which is more work circumcision or healing?
- Jesus tells them to judge rightly.

- Some of the people had heard the leaders wanted to kill Jesus.
- Jesus is bold when He speaks.
- The people want to know if this the Christ.

Things to Ponder:
1. Are you quick to judge others that don't measure up to your religious beliefs?

2. Unbelievers use a form of persecution by pretending you are crazy and hiding their true motives. Do you know how to recognize when people are flipping words and trying to change the reality of what is really going on?

3. How are your boundaries? Can you protect your peace or do others steal it easily?

Challenge: Abuse (aggressive, manipulative, or covert) should not be allowed to have the power to rob you of your peace. Notice when mere words make you struggle to hold your peace. Practice Matthew 10:13-14 with peace robbers. .... Take back your peace of those that aren't worthy of it and Shake the Dust....

Write a prayer and ask God to give you the gift of discernment so you may know when to exercise your empathy and when to let someone else mature through their trials. Psalm 119:125

Day 32

Religious teaching lacks Understanding.

But I know Him...John 7:29

1. What did the Rabbi's teach the people?

John 7:27 NKJV
However, we know where this Man is from; but when the Christ comes, no one knows where He is from."

2. A. Did Jesus come of Himself?

   B. Did these Jews know God, the Father?

John 7:28 NKJV
Then Jesus cried out, as He taught in the temple, saying, "You both know Me, and you know where I am from; and I have not come of Myself, but He who sent Me is true, whom you do not know.

3. Where is Jesus from?

John 7:29 NKJV
But I know Him, for I am from Him, and He sent Me."

4. Could they have ever arrested Jesus and taken Him?

John 7:30 NKJV

Therefore, they sought to take Him; but no one laid a hand on Him, because His hour had not yet come.

5. Many believed in Him. Why?

John 7:31 NKJV
And many of the people believed in Him, and said, "When the Christ comes, will He do more signs than these which this Man has done?"

6. Why were these people murmuring?

* These murmurings made the Pharisees jealous, and they sought to kill Jesus.
John 7:32 NKJV
The Pharisees heard the crowd murmuring these things concerning Him, and the Pharisees and the chief priests sent officers to take Him.

7. Where is Jesus going to go?

John 7:33 NKJV
Then Jesus said to them, "I shall be with you a little while longer, and then I go to Him who sent Me.

8. Who do you think Jesus is talking to when He says, "you cannot come."?

John 7:34 NKJV
You will seek Me and not find Me, and where I am you cannot come."

9. Why would the Pharisees not be able to go where Jesus is going?

John 7:35 NKJV
Then the Jews said among themselves, "Where does He intend to go that we shall not find Him? Does He intend to go to the Dispersion among the Greeks and teach the Greeks?

10. Could the Jews understand?

John 7:36 NKJV
What is this thing that He said, 'You will seek Me and not find Me, and where I am you cannot come'?"

Answers:
1. They taught that no man would know from where the Messiah came from.
2. A. No, Jesus did not come of Himself. B. No, they knew the law of Moses, but the Jews did not know Father, God.
3. Jesus is from God the Father.
4. No, not until the time was right.
5. Many believed in Jesus because of His miracles.
6. The people saw the miracles and were saying isn't this the Christ?
7. Jesus is returning to God, the Father.
8. Jesus is speaking to the Pharisees.
9. The religious leaders are cut off from God because of their lack of belief.
10. No, they did not know He was deity and returning to heaven.

Outline:
- The Rabbi's taught that no one would know where the Christ come from.
- Jesus says that you know Me and where I am from, the problem is that you do not know the Father.
- Jesus is from God the Father.
- They couldn't lay a hand on Jesus before His time.
- Some crowds were for Jesus which made the Pharisees jealous.
- Pharisees are puzzled and jealous when Jesus speaks to them. This made them seek to kill Jesus.
- The religious leaders lacked understanding.

Thought to Ponder:
1. How could you dispel confusion and find direction for your path if you don't understand what God is doing in a circumstance? Proverbs 3:5

2. Trust is like a muscle. What area of your life do you need to move the fear and just simply trust the Lord? Isaiah 41:13

3. Search the Word "Understanding" and outline a few verses: Who gets understanding?

Challenge: Do I have to believe to understand? What is one thing I am to understand? Isaiah 43:10

Write a prayer and ask God for an enlarged heart to increase your understanding. Psalm 119:32

Day 33

Jesus is Living Water

He who believes in Me, ...out of his heart will flow rivers of living water. John 7:38

1. What two things are we to do when we are thirsty?

*Pray to thirst for spiritual growth.
John 7:37 NKJV
On the last day, that great day of the feast, Jesus stood and cried out, saying, "If anyone thirsts, let him come to Me and drink.

2. What is our responsibility if we want "rivers of living water" within us?

John 7:38 NKJV
He who believes in Me, as the Scripture has said, out of his heart will flow rivers of living water."

3. What is the river of living water?

John 7:39 NKJV
But this He spoke concerning the Spirit, whom those believing in Him would receive; for the Holy Spirit was not yet given, because Jesus was not yet glorified.

4. Did many believe?

John 7:40 NKJV
Therefore, many from the crowd when they heard this saying, said, "Truly this is the Prophet."

5. Where did some think He had come from?

John 7:41 NKJV
Others said, "This is the Christ." But some said, "Will the Christ come out of Galilee?

6. Where was Christ born?

John 7:42 NKJV
Has not the Scripture said that the Christ comes from the seed of David and from the town of Bethlehem, where David was?"

7. Did Jesus cause unity or division?

*Jesus did not try to correct the division between people.
John 7:43 NKJV
So, there was a division among the people because of Him.

Answers:
1. The two things: come and drink from the Words of Jesus.
2. We are to believe the Scriptures and then the rivers of living water will be within us.
3. The river of living water is the Holy Ghost that they would receive when Jesus is glorified.
4. Yes, many of them believed.
5. Some thought He was from Galilee.
6. They did not know and did not bother to ask where Jesus was born. Jesus was born in Bethlehem and raised in Nazareth. Matthew 2:1; Matthew 2:23
7. Jesus caused division among the people.

Outline:
- If you are thirsty for truth, come and drink.
- The water of Jesus is living water given by the Holy Spirit.
- Many believed He was a prophet, but questioned where He was from.
- The Christ would come from Bethlehem. Matthew 2:1
- Christ, the Messiah, would be called a Nazarene. Matthew 2:23

Things to Ponder:
1. A person without self-control is just like an ancient city that wasn't fortified with walls for protection. Proverbs 25:28 You can fortify your internal soul with self-control. Name two places in your life that you would like to develop more self-control or self-discipline. This could be as simple as making your bed daily.

2. Following Christ involves moving all confusion and anxiety and building maturity within. Isaiah 60:16 calls our Lord what?

3. Isaiah 60:18 If I take dominion over my own life, I am to allow the Lord to build the walls of my internal city with His Salvation and then do the work to secure the gates of my soul with what?

Challenge: They were walking beside Jesus and struggled to believe. After the Holy Spirit came in the book of Acts, they were walking with Jesus in them and there was a steadfast faithfulness in their walk. They were willing to lay down their lives for Christ. If Jesus is addressing the disciples in every chapter about their unbelief, ask the Holy Spirit where you need to address your unbelief?

Write a prayer and ask the Holy Spirit to come and empower you to believe more. John 1:33; 14:26; 20:22.

Angie Meadows

Day 34

Law can't save.

Does our law judge a man before it hears him...John 7:51

1. A. What did some want to do?

   B. Could they, do it?

John 7:44 NKJV
Now some of them wanted to take Him, but no one laid hands on Him.
*John 10:15-17 Jesus says He lays down His life for the sheep and has the power to take it up again. No one takes His life from him.

2. What did the Pharisees ask the officers?

John 7:45 NKJV
Then the officers came to the chief priests and Pharisees, who said to them, "Why have you not brought Him?"

3. What reason were the officers giving for not arresting Jesus?

John 7:46 NKJV
The officers answered, "No man ever spoke like this Man!"

4. A. What did the Pharisees say to the officers?

   B. Did the leaders believe in Jesus?

John 7:47 NKJV

Book of John

Then the Pharisees answered them, "Are you also deceived?

5. Can you remember any ruler who believed on Jesus? (John 3:1-12)

John 7:48 NKJV
Have any of the rulers or the Pharisees believed in Him?

6. Does the law save? (Rom. 3:19-20; 8:3-5)

John 7:49 NKJV
But this crowd that does not know the law is accursed."

7. Who was one of the rulers who believed in Jesus?

John 7:50 NKJV
Nicodemus (he who came to Jesus by night, being one of them) said to them,

8. What did Nicodemus ask the Pharisees?

John 7:51 NKJV
"Does our law judge a man before it hears him and knows what he is doing?"

9. What was their reasoning/excuse for not believing?

John 7:52 NKJV
They answered and said to him, "Are you also from Galilee? Search and look, for no prophet has arisen out of Galilee."

10. What happened next?

John 7:53 NKJV
And everyone went to his own house.

Answers:
    1. A. Some wanted to arrest Jesus. B. They could not lay hands on Him.

2. Why have you not brought Him?
3. The reason the officers gave for not arresting Jesus was ...Never man spoke like this man.
4. A. They asked are you also deceived? B. No, the leaders did not believe in Jesus.
5. Yes, Nicodemus came to talk to Jesus.
6. No, the law does not save, it only condemns and makes guilty.
7. Nicodemus was Jewish leader who believed.
8. Does our law judge any man before it hears him, and know what he does?
9. They thought Jesus was from Galilee.
10. They all went home.

Outline:
- No one could seize Jesus before His time.
- Officers wouldn't capture Jesus because of the authority in which He spoke.
- The Pharisees mocked anyone who believed as being deceived.
- Following religious laws and rules will not save you.
- Nicodemus was a Jewish ruler and came by night to speak with Jesus.
- Unbelievers will always have an excuse to not believe.
- Maybe unbelievers should just go home.

Thing to Ponder:
1. If you are mocked for following Jesus, is your faith strong enough to disregard them and to continue walking with Christ?

2. If I spend my life following traditions and religious rules without knowing Jesus, will I be saved? Matthew 7:23

3. Matthew 9:12-13 Says Jesus did not come to save the righteous (self-righteous) but the sinner. It is those who are sick who are humble enough to know they need a Savior. How hard is it to admit you need help?

Challenge: What excuses do you hear as to why Jesus isn't the one true Savior? Are these doubts your internal conflicts or of those around you?

Write a prayer and humbly tell the Lord of your doubts and ask Him a question regarding salvation. He is not afraid of your doubts or questions. Write any thoughts that come to you.

John 8

Belief is hearing; hearing is understanding.

"He who is without sin among you, let him throw a stone at her first." John 8:7

Day 35

1. Where did Jesus go next?

John 8:1 NKJV
But Jesus went to the Mount of Olives.

2. Where was Jesus' teaching?

John 8:2 NKJV
Now early in the morning He came again into the temple, and all the people came to Him; and He sat down and taught them.

3. Who brought Jesus the woman taken in adultery?

John 8:3 NKJV
Then the scribes and Pharisees brought to Him a woman caught in adultery. And when they had set her in the midst,

4. What was their accusation of this woman?

Book of John

John 8:4 NKJV
they said to Him, "Teacher, this woman was caught in adultery, in the very act.

5. What does the Law of Moses say should happen to the woman taken in adultery?

John 8:5 NKJV
Now Moses, in the law, commanded us that such should be stoned. But what do You say?"

6. A. Why were they questioning Jesus about this woman?

B. What did Jesus do?

John 8:6 NKJV
This they said, testing Him, that they might have something of which to accuse Him. But Jesus stooped down and wrote on the ground with His finger, as though He did not hear.

7. A. What was their response to this?

B. What did Jesus say to them when He lifted from the ground?

John 8:7 NKJV
So, when they continued asking Him, He raised Himself up and said to them, "He who is without sin among you, let him throw a stone at her first."

8. Then what did Jesus do?

John 8:8 NKJV
And again, He stooped down and wrote on the ground.

9. What convicted them?

John 8:9 NKJV
Then those who heard it, being convicted by their conscience, went out one by one, beginning with the oldest even to the last. And Jesus was left alone, and the woman standing in the midst.

10. A. What happened next?

B. Who was left?

C. What did Jesus say to the woman?

John 8:10 NKJV
When Jesus had raised Himself up and saw no one but the woman, He said to her, "Woman, where are those accusers of yours? Has no one condemned you?"

11. A. What did the woman say?

B. What did Jesus say to her?

John 8:11 NKJV
She said, "No one, Lord." And Jesus said to her, "Neither do I condemn you; go and sin no more."

Answers:
1. Jesus went to the Mount of Olives.
2. Jesus was teaching in the temple.
3. The Scribes and Pharisees brought the woman caught in adultery.
4. Teacher, this woman was caught in adultery.
5. The law says she should be stoned.
6. A. They were tempting Jesus that they might have reason to accuse Him. B. He acted like He didn't hear them and stooped down and wrote on the ground.
7. A. They responded by continuing to ask Him. B. He that is without sin among you, let him first cast a stone at her.
8. Again he stooped down and wrote on the ground.
9. Their own conscience convicted them.
10. They started walking away. B. Only the woman was left. C. Woman, where are those your accusers? Has no one condemned you?
11. A. No man, Lord, is left to condemn me. B. Neither do I condemn you, go, and sin no more.

Outline:
- The place is Mount Olives.
- Jesus is teaching in the temple.
- There is a woman caught in adultery.
- The Pharisees use it as an opportunity to try to trap Jesus.
- The Law says she needed to be stoned.

- Jesus stooped and wrote in the dirt.
- Again, he stooped and wrote in the dirt.
- Their conscience convicted them, and they walked away.
- Woman where are your accusers?
- No one condemns you.
- Go and sin no more.

Things to Ponder:

1. So when Jesus is on the scene, no one has the authority to be an accuser. Let that sink in for a minute. Count how many times you think the worse of others today?

2. How would it feel to know Jesus doesn't condemn you?

3. What would it feel like to go to someone who has stumbled and restore them with a kind word and accountability plan to sin no more?

Challenge: Are you condemning yourself for something you have done in the past or even something someone did to you? Write out Romans 8:1

Write a prayer asking to Lord to release yourself from guilt, shame, and self-condemnation. You simply do this by asking for more grace.

*Guilt, shame, condemnation, negative rumination, or a harsh internal critic is not walking in the Spirit "in" Christ. It is judging yourself harshly under the law and refusing the grace of God.

Book of John

Day 36

Jesus is the light of Life.

He who follows Me shall not walk in darkness but have the light of life. John 8:12

1. What does Jesus say about how you can have light?

John 8:12 NKJV
Then Jesus spoke to them again, saying, "I am the light of the world. He who follows Me shall not walk in darkness but have the light of life."

2. Who is accusing Jesus of bearing record of Himself?

John 8:13 NKJV
The Pharisees therefore said to Him, "You bear witness of Yourself; Your witness is not true."

3. Why does Jesus say His record is true?

John 8:14 NKJV
Jesus answered and said to them, "Even if I bear witness of Myself, my witness is true, for I know where I came from and where I am going; but you do not know where I come from and where I am going.

4. How does Jesus say they judge?

John 8:15 NKJV
You judge according to the flesh; I judge no one.

5. If Jesus judges, why would His judgment be true?

John 8:16 NKJV
And yet if I do judge, my judgment is true; for I am not alone, but I am with the Father who sent Me.

6. How many people should it take to support a testimony?

John 8:17 NKJV
It is also written in your law that the testimony of two men is true.

7. Who are the two that bear witness of Jesus? (John 5:31-37)

John 8:18 NKJV
I am One who bears witness of Myself, and the Father who sent Me bears witness of Me."

8. A. What do the Pharisees ask Jesus?

B. How does Jesus answer them?

C. Did the Pharisees know the Father or recognize Jesus as the Messiah?

John 8:19 NKJV
Then they said to Him, "Where is Your Father?" Jesus answered, "You know neither Me nor My Father. If you had known Me, you would have known My Father also."

9. A. Where was Jesus' teaching?

B. Could any man lay hands on Jesus at this time?

John 8:20 NKJV
These words Jesus spoke in the treasury, as He taught in the temple; and no one laid hands on Him, for His hour had not yet come.

10. Why can't they follow Jesus?

*Unbelief is their greatest sin.
John 8:21 NKJV
Then Jesus said to them again, "I am going away, and you will seek Me, and will die in your sin. Where I go you cannot come."

11. It seems they realize that He is speaking of His death when He is speaking about leaving. So, what do they ask each other?

John 8:22 NKJV
So, the Jews said, "Will He kill Himself, because He says, 'Where I go you cannot come'?"

12. What is Jesus' reason as to why they cannot follow Him?

John 8:23 NKJV
And He said to them, "You are from beneath; I am from above. You are of this world; I am not of this world.

13. What is the reason they are from this world below and dying in their sins? "

John 8:24 NKJV
Therefore, I said to you that you will die in your sins; for if you <u>do not believe</u> that I am He, you will die in your sins."

Answers:
1. Jesus is the light. We must follow Him. Light is life.
2. The Pharisees are accusing Jesus.
3. Jesus says He is true because He knows from where He came and where He will go.
4. They judge after the flesh.
5. Jesus is not alone but would judge with the knowledge of the Father.
6. It takes two people to support a testimony.
7. Jesus bears witness of Himself by agreeing with the Father and the Father bears witness of Him.
8. A. Where is your Father? B. You don't know Me, nor My Father. If you know Jesus, then you know the Father. C. No, the Pharisees did not recognize Jesus's deity.
9. A. He was teaching in the temple where the money was collected. B. No, His hour was not yet come.
10. They can't follow Jesus, because of their sins.
11. Is He going to kill Himself?
12. Jesus tell them they are from beneath.
13. They are dying in their sins because of their unbelief.

Outline:
- Jesus is the light of the world.
- Pharisees don't know the Father, they emphasis religion and not relationship. They are arrogant, false accusers, bullies, and stuck in their unbelief.
- Jesus and the Father bear witness of His sonship.
- You can't know Jesus without knowing the Father.
- No one could take Jesus before His time.
- Unbelievers can't follow Jesus.
- Without believing in Jesus, we will die in our sins.

Things to Ponder:
1. Anxiety, worry, fretfulness, and fearfulness are signs of unbelief? Rate your belief on a scale of 1-10.

2. It is an intentional practice to exercise your trust muscle. What would it look like in your life to trust the Lord with your hardest situations?

3. Lord, give me the gift of faith. I believe and then I forget to believe. Help me.

Challenge: There is a dependency on Jesus that develops faith through the ups and downs of life. How can you intentionally become more dependent upon the Lord. Proverbs 3:5-6

Write a prayer and ask the Lord, to help you recognize when you have forgotten to trust Him.

Angie Meadows

Day 37

Abiding in Jesus

If you abide in My word, you are My disciples indeed. John 8:31

1. Now they are confused, and they ask him, who are you and how did He reply?

John 8:25 NKJV
Then they said to Him, "Who are You?" And Jesus said to them, "Just what I have been saying to you from the beginning.

2. What things does Jesus speak to them?

John 8:26 NKJV
I have many things to say and to judge concerning you, but He who sent Me is true; and I speak to the world those things which I heard from Him."

3. Did the Pharisees understand that Jesus was speaking about the Father?

John 8:27 NKJV
They did not understand that He spoke to them of the Father.

4. What does lift up the Son of Man refer to?

John 8:28 NKJV
Then Jesus said to them, "When you lift up the Son of Man, then you will know that I am He, and that I do nothing of Myself; but as My Father taught Me, I speak these things.

5. A. Has the Father left Jesus alone?

B. Who does Jesus seek to please?

John 8:29 NKJV
And He who sent Me is with Me. The Father has not left Me alone, for I always do those things that please Him."

6. Did Jesus's words change the hearts of some?

John 8:30 NKJV
As He spoke these words, many believed in Him.

7. What did Jesus say to the Jews who believed on Him?

John 8:31 NKJV
Then Jesus said to those Jews who believed Him, "If you abide in My word, you are My disciples indeed.

Answers:
1. Jesus in essence says, I haven't changed. It is the same thing that I have been telling you from the beginning.
2. He speaks to the world of those things which He has heard from God the Father.
3. No, the Pharisees lacked understanding.
4. Jesus being lifted up is a reference to Him dying on the cross.
5. A. No, the Father hasn't left Jesus alone. B. Jesus always seeks to please the Father.
6. Yes, many believed on Him.
7. If you continue, abide, live, dwell in My Word, then you are My disciples.

Outline:
- Jesus doesn't change with the political climate.
- Jesus speaks what He hears the Father say.
- Jesus seeks to please the Father, not the religious leaders.
- Many others around believed as they heard Him speak.
- Abiding (dwelling or living in) the Word of God makes you a strong disciple of Jesus.

Things to Ponder:
1. Can you hold your tongue and pray until you hear the Father speak?

2. If you need more understanding, pray that God would ignite your heart to believe. Understanding comes after believing. Believing is validated through obedience.

3. Write a verse that speaks to your heart and practice abiding in it today.

Challenge: If I am pleasing man, I have stopped pleasing God. Galatians 1:10. What area of my life is skewed because I am trying to please an unpleasable or emotionally immature person?

Write a prayer and ask God for a life verse. A life verse is one that will hold you steady throughout your entire life as you remember God's promises. Mine is *Psalm 17:15 As for me, I will behold Thy face in righteousness; I shall be satisfied, when I awake, with Thy likeness.*

Book of John

Day 38

Truth exposes lies.

...and the truth shall make you free. John 8:32

1. A. If we continue in Jesus's Word, what will we find?

B. What can the truth do for us?

C. What do you think we will be free from?

John 8:32 NKJV
And you shall know the truth, and the truth shall make you free."

2. A. Do the Jews think they are free?

B. Then the Jews ask what question of Jesus?

*Did they forget they were slaves in Egypt? Are they talking about freedom to serve Father, God?
John 8:33 NKJV
They answered Him, "We are Abraham's descendants, and have never been in bondage to anyone. How can You say, 'You will be made free'?"

3. Who is their slave master? (Romans 6:16)

John 8:34 NKJV
Jesus answered them, "Most assuredly, I say to you, whoever commits sin is a slave of sin.

4. Who will abide in his Master's house forever, the servant (slave) or the son?

John 8:35 NKJV
And a slave does not abide in the house forever, but a son abides forever.

5. It is a custom that the son of the master can set a slave free. What will Jesus set us free from?

John 8:36 NKJV
Therefore, if the Son makes you free, you shall be free indeed.

Answers:
1. A. We will know the truth. B. The truth can set us free. C. We will be free from sin.
2. A. Yes, they say, we are Abraham's seed, and were never in bondage to anyone. B. How can you say, you shall be made free?
3. The slave master is sin. Truly we are servants of sin if we commit sin.
4. The son is the one who abides in the house forever.
5. Jesus has the authority and power to set us free from the bondage of sin.

Outline:
- Truth sets us free from lies.
- We can think we are free and be in bondage.
- A key to knowing that I am free is freedom to choose to not sin.
- Freedom from anxiety is to develop the maturity skill of resting in Him.
- Habitual sinning keeps us under the slave master of sin.
- A son abides forever with the father and is heir to all.
- Jesus sets the captives free.

Things to Ponder:
1. If the truth is the opposite of lies, then if I was free wouldn't I be free to follow the truth?

2. True freedom would be the freedom to choose not to sin. So many sins are compelling and addictive. It is important to realize that there is a battle inside of me that needs fought. It is only through the surrender and submission to the Holy Spirit that can keep me from sin. If I am anxious and fearful, I am not free. When I practice

feeling anxious, I am practicing evil and not good. I will find freedom when I repent my way out of anxiety and choose to trust God...no matter what!

Outline this verse:
Romans 7:18-20 NKJV
[18] For I know that in me (that is, in my flesh) nothing good dwells; for to will is present with me, but how to perform what is good I do not find.
- Are we talking about the flesh or spirit?

[19] For the good that I will do, I do not do; but the evil I will not do, that I practice.
- What practical ways could I shift from practicing evil to practicing good?

[20] Now if I do what I will not to do, it is no longer I who do it, but sin that dwells in me.
- What is dwelling in me (in my flesh)?

3. How does Ephesians 2:13 say I can be brought near God?

Challenge: The difference between a slave and a son. The slave in these verses is not free but in bondage to the slave master named sin. The son abides forever with the father and is free not to sin. Name an area of your life where you feel powerless.

Write a prayer and tell Jesus where you are bound and ask Him to set you free.

Book of John

Day 39

Believing=Hearing

Why do you not understand My speech? John 8:43

1. The Jews are Abraham's seed (in the flesh only), how does Jesus know that His Word has no place in them?

John 8:37 NKJV
"I know that you are Abraham's descendants, but you seek to kill Me, because My word has no place in you.

2. Is Jesus saying they have different fathers?

John 8:38 NKJV
I speak what I have seen with My Father, and you do what you have seen with your father."

3. What is their answer and what does Jesus say unto them?

John 8:39 NKJV
They answered and said to Him, "Abraham is our Father." Jesus said to them, "If you were Abraham's children, you would do the works of Abraham.

4. How does Jesus describe Himself?

John 8:40 NKJV
But now you seek to kill Me, a Man who has told you the truth which I heard from God. Abraham did not do this.

5. What deeds are they doing?

*"...not born of fornication" *This could be a dig on His mother Mary who was a virgin that became pregnant through the Holy Spirit before she married Joseph.

John 8:41 NKJV
You do the deeds of your Father." Then they said to Him, "We were not born of fornication; we have one Father-God."

6. Jesus says it cannot be true that God is their Father, why?

John 8:42 NKJV
Jesus said to them, "If God were your Father, you would love Me, for I proceeded forth and came from God; nor have I come of Myself, but He sent Me.

7. Why do the Jews not understand His speech?

John 8:43 NKJV
Why do you not understand My speech? Because you are not able to listen to My word.

Answers:
1. Abraham's descendants are different than Abraham's seed. He knows they are not of God because they seek to kill Him.
2. Jesus says His Father is God. Jesus says they have a different father. His evidence for this is their unbelief, their pride, and their inability to hear truth.
3. They answered, Abraham is our father. Jesus answers them, if you were Abraham's children, you would do the works of Abraham.
4. He describes Himself as a man that has told the truth.
5. They are accusing Him of being born of fornication and doing the deeds of Satan.
6. Because if God were your Father, you would love Me: The ones who truly loved God recognized Jesus as the Messiah.
7 Because they must believe to hear.

Outline:
- Belief is foundational principle set forth in the gospel of John.
- If we indulge, excuse, or rationalize sin, we are in the wrong house and will not find peace.
- Abraham was known for his faith.
- Again, you must believe to have your spiritual ears opened.

Things to Ponder:
1. If you indulge your bitterness it will turn to hatred. Identify anyone you hate. 1 John 3:15; Ephesians 4:26-27

*Often, we just think we are wounded, but if we rehearse this wound it will turn into bitterness and develop a root that will become a stronghold in our life. It takes grace to not be defiled by a wounded heart. Hebrews 12:15

2. The Psalms says I hate those I lie to. So, when you are about to tell a lie to someone you love, remember this isn't love, but hate. Proverbs 26:28 Where do I feel unsafe to tell the truth?

3. How often do we accuse another based upon what we would do, have done or what they have done in the past?

Challenge: Listen to your speech today and stop yourself before you speak hatred (murder), a lie, or accuse another without proof. Confrontation with truth is helping another. Accusations are harming them. Instead, ask questions: what did you mean when you said that? What was your thinking process when you did that? Most people want to do good. Build relationship first and earn the right to speak into others. Now name one relationship you would like to build.

Some principles for **speaking into the life** of another:
1) Are they under my authority?

2) Are they asking for my help?

3) Have I earned their trust?

4) Is there heart ready to receive truth?

5) Do I have any ulterior motives?

6) Is my motive love?

7) Am I judging this person?

8) Will this cause them or anyone else harm?

Standards to **prevent gossip**:
1) Am I part of the problem?

2) Am I part of the solution?

3) Is this any of my business?

Write a prayer and ask the Lord to give you a pure heart and a steadfast spirit. Psalm 51:10

Book of John

Day 40

The Word is Living.

...if anyone keeps My Word, he shall never see death. John 8:51

1. How does Jesus describe the devil?

John 8:44 NKJV
You are of your Father the devil, and the desires of your Father you want to do. He was a murderer from the beginning, and does not stand in the truth, because there is no truth in him. When he speaks a lie, he speaks from his own resources, for he is a liar and the father of it.

2. Why do they not believe Jesus?

John 8:45 NKJV
But because I tell the truth, you do not believe Me.
* Belief activates the hearing ear. A person without the Holy Spirit cannot discern truth.

3. Can any of the Jews convict Jesus of sin?

John 8:46 NKJV
Which of you convicts Me of sin? And if I tell the truth, why do you not believe Me?

4. Why do they not believe Jesus?

John 8:47 NKJV
He who is of God hears God's words; therefore, you do not hear, because you are not of God."

5. What are the new allegations and to whom do they give credit for Jesus's power?

John 8:48 NKJV
Then the Jews answered and said to Him, "Do we not say rightly that You are a Samaritan and have a demon?"

6. A. How does Jesus' answer?

   B. Who does Jesus say He honors?

   C. Who does Jesus say they dishonor?

John 8:49 NKJV
Jesus answered, "I do not have a demon; but I honor My Father, and you dishonor Me.

7. Does Jesus seek His own glory?

John 8:50 NKJV
And I do not seek My own glory; there is One who seeks and judges.

8. How is it that we can never see spiritual death?

John 8:51 NKJV
Most assuredly, I say to you, if anyone keeps My Word, he shall never see death."

Answers:
1. Satan is a murderer. There is no truth in him because he is a liar, and the father of lies.
2. They cannot hear truth because they belong to the father of lies and do not believe in Jesus.
3. No, none of the Jews can find any sin in Jesus.
4. You cannot hear God's Words if you are not of God.
5. They call Him a Samaritan. They say His power is from demons.
6. A. Jesus answers and says I do not have a devil. B. Jesus says He honors His Father, God. C. The Jews dishonor God the Father with their dishonor of the Son, Jesus.
7. No, Jesus seeks only to glorify the Father.
8. If we keep the sayings of Jesus, we will never spiritually die.

Outline:
- Satan is a murderer, father of lies (with no truth in him).

Book of John

- When we align ourselves with a lie, we cannot hear truth.
- There is no sin in Jesus. He was without sin. Hebrews 4:15
- If Jesus was persecuted how much more will they persecute us. John 15:20
- A person who doesn't believe in the one true God will not believe Jesus.
- The goal of the life of the believer is to glorify God.
- Jesus is the Word of life, in Him is no death.

Things to Ponder:
1. How do you react when others falsely accuse you?

2. When you are internally dysregulated, do you stuff it, stew on it, or spew it?

Instead, how could you practice being steadfast? 1 Corinthians 15:58

3. Can you not condemn yourself but instead extend yourself grace and honor God?

Challenge: In Acts 5:17-20 the apostles were falsely accused. What was the angel's instructions in verse 20 to the apostles?

If you are the temple of God, what would it look like to stand and speak life to yourself? 1 Corinthians 3:17

Write a prayer and ask God for the supernatural ability to preach to yourself. This is a life skill to redeem yourself from any pit with the promises of God and the Words of Life.

Day 41

I am that I am.

...before Abraham was, I AM. John 8:58

1. What type of death did the Jews think He was talking about a physical death or a spiritual death?

John 8:52 NKJV
Then the Jews said to Him, "Now we know that You have a demon! Abraham is dead, and the prophets; and You say, 'If anyone keeps My Word, he shall never taste death.'

2. Now they want to know if He is greater than whom?

John 8:53 NKJV
Are You greater than our Father Abraham, who is dead? And the prophets are dead. Who do You make Yourself out to be?"

3. A. Who honors Jesus?

   B. Who does the Jews say is their God?

John 8:54 NKJV
Jesus answered, "If I honor Myself, My honor is nothing. It is My Father who honors Me, of whom you say that He is your God.

4. Does Jesus say they know the Father?

John 8:55 NKJV
Yet you have not known Him, but I know Him. And if I say, 'I do not know Him,' I shall be a liar like you; but I do know Him and keep His word.

5. Does Jesus say Abraham knew of His coming?

John 8:56 NKJV
Your Father Abraham rejoiced to see My day, and he saw it and was glad."

6. Now what do the Jews want to know?

John 8:57 NKJV
Then the Jews said to Him, "You are not yet fifty years old, and have You seen Abraham?"

7. What is Jesus' answer? (John 1:1-5).

John 8:58 NKJV
Jesus said to them, "Most assuredly, I say to you, before Abraham was, I AM."

8. A. Why did the Jews want to stone Him?

B. Could they stone Him? "

*"I am" is a reference to Jesus being deity. He was telling them He was God in the flesh.
John 8:59 NKJV
Then they took up stones to throw at Him; but Jesus hid Himself and went out of the temple, going through the midst of them, and so passed by.

Answers:
1. The Jews thought He was talking about a physical death.
2. The Jewish leaders want to know if Jesus is greater than Abraham and the prophets.
3. A. God the Father honors Jesus. B. The Jews say that God the Father is their God.
4. No, He says they do not know God the Father.
5. Yes, Jesus says, Abraham rejoiced to see My day.
6. How could Abraham have saw You? You are not even 50 years old yet.
7. Jesus makes a profound statement and says before Abraham was, I AM. He is telling them He was from the beginning of time.

8. A. They wanted to stone Jesus because He was telling them He was God in the flesh. B. No, they couldn't stone Him, He hid himself and then walked right through the midst of them and passed by.

Outline:
- There is a physical and a spiritual death.
- There is a time to be prudent and hide yourself from evil. Proverbs 22:3
- God honors the Son, Jesus.
- Those who don't believe in Jesus, do not know the Father.
- The Lord showed Abraham His plans (Genesis 26:4).
- "I AM" is the name God gave Himself when He spoke to Moses from the burning bush. So, when Jesus said He was "I AM", they considered it blasphemy. (Exodus 3:14)
- No one could take Jesus or hurt Him or do anything until it was time for Him to lay down His life willingly. (John 10:15-18)

Things to Ponder:
1. Do you know how to speak a blessing over yourself?

2. Do you know how to preach to yourself?

3. Do you know the great I AM? Does He burn in your heart? Luke 24:32

Challenge: If I focus on my fickle emotions, I will have a rotten day. If I focus on the unchanging Word of God, I will land on solid ground. *Jesus Christ is the same yesterday, today and forever. Hebrews 13:8* Jesus is the solid rock. My anxiety is quicksand and giving my power away to something inferior.

Now find a verse to preach to yourself today. Rehearse it 100 times if necessary to break any negative thought patterns. Rehearse this verse instead of your anxiety.

Write a prayer and ask God to know Him as steadfast strength and to show you something about His love that you do not know. Write what you hear.

John 9

Jesus is the Light

I am the light of the world. John 9:5

Day 42

1. Who does Jesus' pass by?

John 9:1 NKJV
Now as Jesus passed by, He saw a man who was blind from birth.

2. What did His disciples ask Him?

John 9:2 NKJV
And His disciples asked Him, saying, "Rabbi, who sinned, this man or his parents, that he was born blind?"

3. What is one of the reasons for deformities and illness?

John 9:3 NKJV
Jesus answered, "Neither this man nor his parents sinned, but that the works of God should be revealed in him.

4. Whose works is Jesus doing?

John 9:4 NKJV
I must work the works of Him who sent Me while it is day; the night is coming when no one can work.

5. How is Jesus describing Himself? John 8:12

John 9:5 NKJV
As long as I am in the world, I am the light of the world."

6. What did Jesus do next?

John 9:6 NKJV
When He had said these things, He spat on the ground and made clay with the saliva; and He anointed the eyes of the blind man with the clay.

7. A. What was Jesus's command to the blind man?

   B. Did the man obey?

*We always have responsibility to hear, believe and obey.
John 9:7 NKJV
And He said to him, "Go, wash in the pool of Siloam" (which is translated, Sent). So, he went and washed, and came back seeing.

Answers:
1. Jesus passed by a man who was blind from his birth.
2. The disciples asked, who was the sinner? This man or his parents.
3. One of reasons for illness and deformities is that the works of God should be made manifest.
4. Jesus is doing the work of God the Father.
5. Jesus describes Himself as the light of the world.
6. Jesus spat on the ground and made clay and He anointed the eyes of the blind man.
7. A. Jesus commanded the blind man to go wash in the pool of Siloam. B. Yes, and the blind man obeyed, then he came seeing.

Outline:
- There are misunderstandings around sickness and disease.
- God wants to heal.
- Jesus came to do the work of the Father.
- Jesus is the light of the world.
- Jesus healed differently on different occasions. There is no formula for healing.
- It is our responsibility to hear, believe and obey.

Things to Ponder:
1. What would it look like in your life to meditate upon the Word of the Lord (and not your fickle emotions) to self-regulate and emotionally balance yourself? *This is a spiritual maturity skill.

2. Think of a situation that is broke and you do not know how to fix it, then shift, and focus on doing what you do know to do in another area of life. What is the broken thing? What is the thing you know is good and healthy to do?

3. Release the broken thing to the Lord now.

Challenge: Ask counsel of those who are confident enough to disagree with you and close enough to the Lord to tell you what the Word says. Name one trusted friend.

Write a prayer and ask God for a trusted friend. A trusted friend may still disappoint but will be safe to go to and work out any conflicts or disappointments. They will apologize quickly without offense to heal any division in the relationship. This is a trusted friend.

Day 43

Jesus causes division

...And there was a division among them. John 9:16

1. What did the neighbors say?

John 9:8 NKJV
Therefore, the neighbors and those who previously had seen that he was blind said, "Is not this he who sat and begged?"

2. What did the beggar say?

John 9:9 NKJV
Some said, "This is he." Others said, "He is like him." He said, "I am he."

3. What did they ask the formally blind beggar?

John 9:10 NKJV
Therefore, they said to him, "How were your eyes opened?"

4. A. What did the man answer them?

   B. What does the blind man describe next?

* If we want our spiritual eyes open, then we must trust the Words of Jesus and obey to our best ability.
John 9:11 NKJV
He answered and said, "A Man called Jesus made clay and anointed my eyes and said to me, 'Go to the pool of Siloam and wash.' So, I went and washed, and I received sight."

5. Who do the people want to meet now?

*When people see you with a changed heart and a changed life, they will want to meet Jesus.
John 9:12 NKJV
Then they said to him, "Where is He?" He said, "I do not know."

6. What did these neighbors do next?

John 9:13 NKJV
They brought him who formerly was blind to the Pharisees.

7. What day of the week was it?

*The Jews had many man-made religious rules.
John 9:14 NKJV
Now it was a Sabbath when Jesus made the clay and opened his eyes.

8. What questions did the Pharisees ask the formerly blind beggar?

John 9:15 NKJV
Then the Pharisees also asked him again how he had received his sight. He said to them, "He put clay on my eyes, and I washed, and I see."

9. What was the division of the Pharisees?

* It never occurred to the Pharisees that their rules on the Sabbath could be wrong.
John 9:16 NKJV
Therefore, some of the Pharisees said, "This Man is not from God, because He does not keep the Sabbath." Others said, "How can a man who is a sinner do such signs?" And there was a division among them.

10. Who did the blind man say Jesus was?

John 9:17 NKJV

They said to the blind man again, "What do you say about Him because He opened your eyes?" He said, "He is a prophet."

Answers:
1. The neighbors said is this the beggar?
2. The beggar said, yes, it is me.
3. The people asked how can you see?
4. A. The healed man answered and said a man that is called Jesus made clay, and anointed mine eyes, and said unto me, Go to the pool of Siloam, and wash: B. The blind man describes his obedience to Jesus.
5. When you become a new person, people will want to meet the Jesus that healed you.
6. The neighbors took the healed man to the Pharisees.
7. It was the Sabbath Day.
8. The Pharisees directed questions to the healed blind man.
9. This man (Jesus) cannot be of God He does not keep the Sabbath.
10. The blind man said Jesus was a prophet.

Outline:
- Beggars can be chosen to be healed.
- Blindness did not negate the blind man's responsibility to follow instructions.
- The people wanted to meet the miracle worker.
- The Pharisees had so many rules about the Sabbath that they couldn't fathom God caring more about a person than a religious rule.
- The Sabbath is for man, not man for the Sabbath Mark 2:27. Luke 6:5 and Matthew 12:8 says the Son of Man is Lord over the Sabbath. *Jesus is greater than the religious rules.
- Even though Jesus opened the blind man's physical eyes He did not see spiritually and could not discern Jesus as Messiah. He thought Jesus was a prophet.

Things to Ponder:
1. Are there religious traditions you follow as rules?

2. Have you been obedient to everything you feel like the Lord has told you to do?

3. Can you tolerate differing view on the Sabbath and other things that are not a salvation issue?

Challenge: The fourth commandment is to Observe the Sabbath Day and keep it holy. Ponder your thoughts on the Sabbath. What would it mean to you to keep it holy?

Write a prayer and ask God to give you wisdom and show you any area of your life that may be hindering your spiritual growth.

Day 44

Miracles Questioned

...because they feared the Jews, John 9:22

1. The Jews did not believe that the man had been blind, so what did they do?

John 9:18 NKJV
But the Jews did not believe concerning him, that he had been blind and received his sight, until they called the parents of him who had received his sight.

2. What two questions did the Pharisees ask the parents?

John 9:19 NKJV
And they asked them, saying, "Is this your son, who you say was born blind? How then does he now see?"

3. How do the parents answer?

*The parents state the facts.
John 9:20 NKJV
His parents answered them and said, "We know that this is our son, and that he was born blind.

4. What do the parents say next?

John 9:21 NKJV
but by what means he now sees we do not know, or who opened his eyes we do not know. He is of age; ask him. He will speak for himself."

5. A. Why did the parents speak these words?

B. What was the consequence to be if someone believed that Jesus was the Christ?

John 9:22 NKJV
His parents said these things because they feared the Jews, for the Jews had agreed already that if anyone confessed that He was Christ, he would be put out of the synagogue.

6. Do you think the parents were bold?

John 9:23 NKJV
Therefore, his parents said, "He is of age; ask him."

Answers:
1. The Jews called the man's parents.
2. Is this your son, who was born blind? How is it that he now sees?
3. When questioned the parents just said, we know that this is our son, who was born blind.
4. The parents answered, we don't know how his eyes got opened. Ask him, he is an adult.
5. A. The parents were afraid of the Jews. B. Believers in Christ were to be put out of the synagogue.
6. No, the parents were not bold.

Outline:
- Others may not believe your miracle.
- Others may try to trap you in your words.
- Even your support system may be afraid to have your back.
- Your own endearing parents may throw you under the bus.
- Religious and political leaders may make us cower with fear of rejection.
- To be an outcast for our beliefs can be rough.
- It takes boldness to know and speak the truth.

Things to Ponder:
1. Do you have anyone who will speak in your behalf?

2. Have you been persecuted for your beliefs?

3. Is your spiritual insight growing and changing as you mature in Christ?

Challenge: If you believe exactly like you believed a decade ago, ask the Lord to challenge and expand your understanding in any area He chooses. And then prepare yourself to listen over the next week or so.

Write a prayer and ask God in what ways He wants to deliver you from the fear of persecution and be your comforter, provider, and protector? Listen and write what you hear.

Book of John

Day 45

Jesus opens the eyes of the blind.

...I was blind, now I see. John 9:25

1. A. What did the Pharisees say to the healed man?

   B. Who are the Pharisees calling a sinner?

John 9:24 NKJV
So, they again called the man who was blind, and said to him, "Give God the glory! We know that this Man is a sinner."

2. What is the one thing the man claims to know for sure?

John 9:25 NKJV
He answered and said, "Whether He is a sinner or not I do not know. One thing I know: that though I was blind, now I see."

*When our spiritual eyes are opened, we will not be able to answer all their questions. But we will know that we are able to see the Word of God with new eyes.

3. What are the Pharisees doing?

John 9:26 NKJV
Then they said to him again, "What did He do to you? How did He open your eyes?"

4. What answering technique did the man use on the Pharisees?

John 9:27 NKJV
He answered them, "I told you already, and you did not listen. Why do you want to hear it again? Do you also want to become His disciples?"

5. When the Pharisees could not get the answer they wanted, they resorted to what?

*Revile means to be subjected to abusive language.
John 9:28 NKJV
Then they reviled him and said, "You are His disciple, but we are Moses' disciples.

6. What confusing tactics are the Pharisees using now?

*They are speaking truth, then adding a confusing statement.

John 9:29 NKJV
We know that God spoke to Moses; as for this fellow, we do not know where He is from."

7. What was the healed man's courageous speech?

John 9:30 NKJV
The man answered and said to them, "Why, this is a marvelous thing, that you do not know where He is from; yet He has opened my eyes!

8. What is he saying Jesus would have to be doing for God to use Him to heal him?

*The healed man is defending Jesus.
John 9:31 NKJV
Now we know that God does not hear sinners; but if anyone is a worshiper of God and does His will, He hears him.

9. Now what question/statement is the healed man making in his speech?

John 9:32 NKJV
Since the world began it has been unheard of that anyone opened the eyes of one who was born blind.

10. What kind of rational defense is the healed man making now?

*See Isaiah 35:5
John 9:33 NKJV
If this Man were not from God, He could do nothing."

11. A. Is this man able to teach the proud Pharisees anything?

B. What reasons do they give this man that he cannot teach them?

C. What was this man's crime that got him cast out?

John 9:34 NKJV
They answered and said to him, "You were completely born in sins, and are you teaching us?" And they cast him out.

Answers:

1. A. Give God the glory for your healing. B. Then the Pharisees called Jesus a sinner.
2. The formerly blind man says... I know I was blind, but now I see.
3. The Pharisees seems to be interrogating and asking the same questions over again.
4. He explained to them that obviously they could not hear him. Then he asked them a question.
5. They reviled him and justified themselves by saying they were Moses' disciples.
6. We know that God spoke unto Moses (truth). As for this fellow, we do not know where He comes from (confusion).
7. This is a marvelous thing that this man, Jesus, opened my eyes and yet you cannot figure it out.
8. Jesus would need to be a worshipper of God and doing God's will for Him to be able to heal.
9. Since the world began has anyone opened the eyes of the blind.
10. Opening the eyes of the blind would be the work of God.
11. A. No, you cannot teach a proud man much of anything. B. They revert to their false beliefs and say that he was born in sins because he was born blind. C. He was being honest and speaking his true convictions which disagreed with the Pharisees' religious beliefs.

Outline:
- Give God the glory for healing.
- Religious leaders that did not understand that God was doing a new thing, verbally rejected what they did not understand.
- Religious leaders seemed to like twisting words, reviling others, and falsely accusing someone who was innocent.
- Religious leaders cling to traditions.
- When your physically healed or you are spiritually awakened do not let anyone take it from you because they don't believe your experience.
- Stick to what you know is true.
- Worshippers do the will of the Father.
- Proud men are blind and cling to their false beliefs.

Things to Ponder:
1. If we exam John 14:12, what will we be doing? Do you think we will be able to open the eyes of the blind?

2. Where is God calling you to make a difference?

3. Do you know how to "wait" on the Lord for His timing? Sometimes a work is in your heart for decades before the Lord opens doors. Just pray it down, until the Lord strengthens your heart to believe. Psalm 27:14

Challenge: Are you resisting change and clinging to the familiar? Could the Lord be doing a new thing? Isaiah 43:19

Write a prayer and ask God to strengthen your heart and you make your path plain before you. Psalm 27:11

Day 46

Believers respond with Worship.

"Lord, I believe!" And he worshiped Him. John 9:38

1. A. Who came looking for him when he was cast out?

   B. What did Jesus ask him?

John 9:35 NKJV
Jesus heard that they had cast him out; and when He had found him, He said to him, "Do you believe in the Son of God?"

2. Did the man recognize Jesus?

John 9:36 NKJV
He answered and said, "Who is He, Lord, that I may believe in Him?"

3. What was Jesus' answer?

John 9:37 NKJV
And Jesus said to him, "You have both seen Him and it is He who is talking with you."

4. A. Did the man believe?

   B. What do believers do?

John 9:38 NKJV
Then he said, "Lord, I believe!" And he worshiped Him.

5. Can you make sense out of what Jesus is saying?

John 9:39 NKJV
And Jesus said, "For judgment I have come into this world, that those who do not see may see, and that those who see may be made blind."

6. What does the Pharisees ask Jesus?

John 9:40 NKJV
Then some of the Pharisees who were with Him heard these words, and said to Him, "Are we blind also?"

7. What does Jesus answer them?

John 9:41 NKJV
Jesus said to them, "If you were blind, you would have no sin; but now you say, 'We see.' Therefore, your sin remains.
*This may indicate that people who are ignorant of truth and are seeking and asking for God to reveal truth may not be liable for their sin. But if they are self-righteous and saying they know it all when they don't... they are responsible.

Answers:
1. A. Jesus came looking for him. B. Do you believe on the Son of God?
2. No, he didn't recognize Jesus because he was blind when he was previously near Jesus.
3. Jesus answered, you have both seen Him, and it is He that talks with you.
4. A. Yes, the man believed. B. When we believe we worship Jesus.
5. I have come so that the blind can see and to show those who think they can see that they are blind.
6. The Pharisees asked, are you saying we are blind?
7. Jesus answers, if you were blind (ignorant) you would have no sin: but since you refuse to see, your sin remains.

Outline:
- Jesus came looking for the healed blind man who the Pharisees cast out.
- The man had been blind and didn't recognize Jesus.
- Jesus reveals to this healed blind man that He is the Son of God.
- The healed man believed. *Miracles are to help us believe.

Things to Ponder:

1. Did your spiritual eyes open all at once or has it been a gradual opening?

2. Do you have co-workers or family members who are divisive and cause you to respond in fear and not faith?

3. Practice non-emotional responses today with others. *Emotions can be easily manipulated by others.
Your instructions are to stand bold. Expect persecution vs. 35 and then let Jesus find you and allow Him to comfort you vs. 39. Do you get stuck in the injustice and resist comfort?

Divisive Tactics	Righteous Defense
Relying on man-made rules vs. 16	Speak what you know for certain vs. 17.
Calling witness and bullying others vs.18-19	State the facts vs. 25
Calling good evil vs. 24	Answering with a question vs. 27
Asking the same question over and over vs. 26	Speak boldly vs. 30
Reviling, accusing & justifying self vs. 28	Defend Jesus vs. 31
Mixing truth with error to cause confusion vs. 29	Speak of the awesome power of God vs. 32
Unable to be taught because of unbelief vs. 34	Make a rational defense vs. 33

Challenge: Follow the steps and practice a righteous defense.

Write a prayer about a situation in your life that seems unresolvable and ask Jesus to come and comfort you. Now sit quietly and open your heart. Ask the Lord to reveal to you any wound that is blocking you from receiving Him.

John 10

The Good Shepherd

...and the sheep hear his voice; John 10:3

Day 47

1. **Verily, verily, or truly, truly** means doubly sure I say unto you. It expresses complete authority. A **sheepfold** is a low building open at the top surrounded by stone wall or fence and a layer of thorns on top. It has a guarded door and is a place to rest at night safely.

What is the character of a thief?

*A thief also refers to a false guide who does not care to instruct people but abuses their confidence for gain.
John 10:1 NKJV
"Most assuredly, I say to you, he who does not enter the sheepfold by the door, but climbs up some other way, the same is a thief and a robber.

2. Who enters through the door of the sheepfold?

John 10:2 NKJV
But he who enters by the door is the shepherd of the sheep.

3. A. Who is the porter?

B. Do the sheep recognize the voice of their shepherd?

C. Why do the sheep follow the shepherd?

*Shepherds will even name their sheep and the sheep respond to their name.
John 10:3 NKJV
To him the doorkeeper opens, and the sheep hear his voice; and he calls his own sheep by name and leads them out.

4. A. Who leads the sheep?

B. Why do the sheep follow the shepherd?

John 10:4 NKJV
And when he brings out his own sheep, he goes before them; and the sheep follow him, for they know his voice.

5. Will the sheep follow a stranger?

John 10:5 NKJV
Yet they will by no means follow a stranger, but will flee from him, for they do not know the voice of strangers.

6. What is a parable?

*It is a short fictitious story that illustrates a moral attitude or a religious principle.
John 10:6 NKJV
Jesus used this illustration, but they did not understand the things which He spoke to them.

Answers:
1. **Thief** is a robber who often uses violence or bullying to get his way.
2. A true shepherd enters the gate.
3. A. The keeper of the gate and protector of the sheep at night is called a porter.
B. Yes, sheep learn to recognize the voice of their shepherd. C. The sheep have learned to trust the shepherd to care for them.

4. A. The shepherd leads the sheep. B. The sheep will follow the voice they know.
5. No, the sheep will not know a stranger's voice.
6. Parables are described as a heavenly story with an earthly meaning.

Outline:
- Thieves pretend to be shepherds.
- Thieves use violence.
- Shepherds are transparent and accountable to others.
- Shepherds are protectors.
- Sheep will not trust or follow a stranger.
- Shepherds will lead the sheep.
- Parables are heavenly stories with earthly meanings.

Things to Ponder:
1. Who are the thieves in your life that come to you through illegitimate means?

2. Name your shepherds who are your protectors and defenders?

3. Who do you shepherd?

Challenge: Find a person in your life (child, teenager, co-worker, neighbor, spouse) that is attentive to you and gently guide them with tenderness, patience, and love to train them to do one task. Repeat this task until they are confident with it. Investment in others is key to relationship stability.

Book of John

Write a prayer and ask God for deep and rich love for others. Others will feel loved when I am patient and kind. Practice patience and kindness. 1 Corinthians 13:4

Day 48

Jesus is the door.

I am the good shepherd. John 10:11

1. Jesus describes Himself as what?

John 10:7 NKJV
Then Jesus said to them again, "Most assuredly, I say to you, I am the door of the sheep.

2. Will the sheep hear a false Messiah?

John 10:8 NKJV
All who ever came before Me are thieves and robbers, but the sheep did not hear them.

3. If we go through the door and are in Jesus, what is the promise?

*Sheep with a shepherd are fed and safe.
John 10:9 NKJV
I am the door. If anyone enters by Me, he will be saved, and will go in and out and find pasture.

4. A. What is the purpose of the thief?

B. For what purpose did Jesus come?

John 10:10 NKJV
The thief does not come except to steal, and to kill, and to destroy. I have come that they may have life, and that they may have it more abundantly.

5. What will a good shepherd do for His sheep?

John 10:11 NKJV
"I am the good shepherd. The good shepherd gives His life for the sheep."

6. What will a person hired to take care of the sheep do when a wolf comes?

John 10:12 NKJV
But a hireling, he who is not the shepherd, one who does not own the sheep, sees the wolf coming and leaves the sheep and flees; and the wolf catches the sheep and scatters them.

7. Why would a hireling flee?

John 10:13 NKJV
The hireling flees because he is a hireling and does not care about the sheep.

Answers:
1. Jesus describes himself as the door for the sheep to enter in.
2. No, the sheep will not hear a false shepherd.
3. If we are "in" Jesus, we shall be saved and shall go in and out and find pasture.
4. A. The thief's purpose is to steal, to kill and to destroy (purpose of Satan). B. Jesus wants to give us life that we might have it more abundantly.
5. A good shepherd will give his life to protect his sheep.
6. The sheep that do not belong to the hired shepherd will flee and let the wolf catch the flock or scatter them.
7. A hireling would flee because he does not care for the sheep.

Outline:
- Jesus is the door for the sheep.
- True sheep will not hear thieves and robbers.
- Jesus is the gate.
- There is safe pasture in Jesus.
- The thief will kill, steal, and destroy.
- A true shepherd will lay his life down for his sheep.
- A hired shepherd will let the flock scatter and be devoured.
- A hired shepherd will run.

Thoughts to Ponder:
1. When the going gets tough, do you run? Have you abandoned a child who needed your protection?

2. What situation in your life do you need steadfast perseverance to continue to move forward?

3. Tell me how you lay down your life (wants & desires) for your loved ones?

Challenges: Can you name the things in your life (thieves) that have come to kill, steal, and destroy your dreams and destiny?

Write a prayer and ask God to restore something to you that has been stolen.

Day 49

Jesus listens to the Father's Commands.

My Father loves Me. John 10:17

1. Who does Jesus say He is?

John 10:14 NKJV
I am the good shepherd; and I know My sheep and am known by My own.

2. Who does Jesus lay His life down for?

John 10:15 NKJV
As the Father knows Me, even so I know the Father; and I lay down My life for the sheep.

3. A. Will there be other sheep not of this fold (not Jews)?

   B. Will the sheep (Jews) and the other sheep (Gentiles) be in one-fold with one shepherd?

John 10:16 NKJV
And other sheep I have which are not of this fold; them also I must bring, and they will hear My voice; and there will be one flock and one shepherd.

4. Why does the Father love Jesus?

John 10:17 NKJV
"Therefore, My Father loves Me, because I lay down My life that I may take it again.

5. A. Will anyone be able to take Jesus's life from Him?

B. Does Jesus have the power to take His life back again?

John 10:18 NKJV
No one takes it from Me, but I lay it down of Myself. I have power to lay it down, and I have power to take it again. This command I have received from My Father."

6.   What did Jesus's teaching do?

John 10:19 NKJV
Therefore, there was a division again among the Jews because of these sayings.

Answers:
1. I am the good shepherd.
2. Jesus lays down His life for the sheep.
3. A. Yes, Jesus says there will be other sheep in His fold. B. Yes, Jesus says it will be one shepherd and one-fold.
4. The Father loves Jesus because He will lay down His life for the sheep.
5. A. No, He will willingly lay it down. B. Yes, Jesus has the power to take His life back.
6. Jesus's teaching causes division.

Outline:
- Jesus' sheep know Him.
- Jesus laid down His life for His sheep.
- Jesus is known by the Father.
- Other sheep belong to Jesus too (not Jews, but Gentiles).
- Jesus will lay down His life and take it up again.
- This New Testament way caused division.

Things to Ponder:
1. Is Jesus doing a new thing in your life?

2. Where is there division in your life?

3. Is it division because of the thief? Or division because of a new thing?

Challenge: What important goals have you established in this season of your life? Write out three goals.

Write a prayer and ask God to help you go to the mountain (a quiet place) to refine your focus. Write what you hear.

Day 50

Unbelief causes deafness.

Can a demon open the eyes of the blind? John 10:21

1. What did part of the people say?

John 10:20 NKJV
And many of them said, "He has a demon and is mad. Why do you listen to Him?"

2. What did the other people say?

John 10:21 NKJV
Others said, "These are not the words of one who has a demon. Can a demon open the eyes of the blind?"

3. What time of year was it?

John 10:22 NKJV
Now it was the Feast of Dedication in Jerusalem, and it was winter.

4. Where was Jesus?

*This was the porch that was 800ft long and faced the east side. It was built by Solomon.
John 10:23 NKJV
And Jesus walked in the temple, in Solomon's porch.

5. What are the Jews asking Jesus?

John 10:24 NKJV
Then the Jews surrounded Him and said to Him, "How long do You keep us in doubt? If You are the Christ, tell us plainly."

6. A. Has Jesus already told them He was the Messiah?

   B. Did they believe Him?

   C. Does Jesus do anything in His own name?

John 10:25 NKJV
Jesus answered them, "I told you, and you do not believe. The works that I do in My Father's name, they bear witness of Me.

7. Why do they not believe?

John 10:26 NKJV
But you do not believe, because you are not of My sheep, as I said to you.

Answers:
1. He has a devil and is mad. We should not listen to Him.
2. These are not the works of a devil.
3. It was in the winter at the time of the Feast of Dedication.
4. He was in the temple on Solomon's porch.
5. They are asking Jesus to tell them plainly if He is the Messiah.
6. A. Yes, Jesus told them He was the Messiah. B. No, they didn't believe Him. C. No, Jesus does nothing without direction from the Father.
7. These Jews cannot believe in Jesus because they are not His sheep.

Outline:
- Jesus is falsely accused.
- Jesus can open the eyes of the blind, demons cannot.
- The time of the year is winter and the Feast of Dedication.
- Jesus was in the temple on Solomon's porch.
- The people asked questions that they were not ready to believe the true answers.
- Jesus' works bore witness of His authority through the Father.
- Those that do not belong to Jesus cannot hear Him.

Thoughts to Ponder:

1. How do you respond when you are personally attacked?

2. How easily can you distance and detach yourself emotionally from toxic people?

3. How secure and confident are you in Christ?

Challenge: If I am following God, I can expect persecution. How can I be prepared and practice holding my own peace?

Write a prayer and recognize persecution and ask for the blessing of the kingdom of heaven promised in Matthew 5:10 for those who are persecuted.

Book of John

Day 51

Jesus and the Father are one.

My Father, is greater than all; John 10:29

1. A. Who does Jesus know?

   B. Can the sheep recognize the voice of Jesus?

   C. How can we identify true sheep?

John 10:27 NKJV
My sheep hear My voice, and I know them, and they follow Me.

2. A. What is the promise for those that follow Jesus?

   B. Could any man take the sheep from Jesus?

John 10:28 NKJV
And I give them eternal life, and they shall never perish; neither shall anyone snatch them out of My hand.

3. A. Who gave the sheep to Jesus?

   B. Who is greater than all?

   C. Can anyone snatch the sheep out of the Father's hand?

John 10:29 NKJV
My Father, who has given them to Me, is greater than all; and no one is able to snatch them out of My Father's hand.

4. Who is one with the Father?

John 10:30 NKJV
I and My Father are one."

5. When Jesus said He and the Father are one, what was the reaction from the Jews?

John 10:31 NKJV
Then the Jews took up stones again to stone Him.

6. Jesus asks them what is My crime?

John 10:32 NKJV
Jesus answered them, "Many good works I have shown you from My Father. For which of those works do you stone Me?"

7. What did the Jews answer?

John 10:33 NKJV
The Jews answered Him, saying, "For a good work we do not stone You, but for blasphemy, and because You, being a Man, make Yourself God."

Answers:
1. A. Jesus knows His sheep. B. Yes, sheep recognize the voice of their shepherd. C. They will follow Jesus.
2. A. The promise is eternal life. B. No one or nothing can take you from Jesus.
3. A. The Father gave the sheep to Jesus. B. The Father is greater than all. C. No, no one, can pluck you from the Father's hand.
4. Jesus is one with the Father.
5. They took up stones to stone Him (again).
6. Many good works have I showed you from My Father; for which of those works do you stone Me?
7. We do not stone You for good works, we stone You for blasphemy. Blaspheme means to revile, abuse or be irreverent to God.

Book of John

Outline:
- There is one shepherd and one-fold; the Jews and Gentiles are together.
- Jewish leaders cannot believe Jesus because they aren't His sheep.
- Sheep will hear the true shepherd's voice and follow.
- Promise is eternal life. We are safe "in" Jesus.
- No one can pluck you out of the hand of the Father.
- Jesus and the Father are one.
- The little "g" gods are those who hear the Word of God.
- Jesus is the Word.
- Jesus addresses unbelief.
- Those who follow Jesus---believe.

Things to Ponder:
1. Is your belief strong enough to feel the divinity of God within yourself? The Lord's presence is evident by peace.

2. If God is love, how can I rely more on His love? Write 1 John 4:16.

3. Do you identify with past traumas, current troubles or with the love of God for you? *Sit quietly and listen to your passive thoughts to hear this answer.

Challenges: When we find love, we will find God. What in your attitude isn't of love and needs corrected?

Write a prayer and ask the Lord to show you what leader (pastor, boss, teacher, police officer) in your life needs your encouragement? Send the text, email, or note of encouragement.

Book of John

Day 52

Receiving the Word makes us little gods.

And many believed in Him there. John 10:42

1. Jesus refers to an Old Testament Psalm 82:6. What is their double standard?

John 10:34 NKJV
Jesus answered them, "Is it not written in your law, 'I said, "You are gods"'?

2. Who did the Old Testament psalmist call gods?

John 10:35 NKJV
If He called them gods, to whom the word of God came (and the Scripture cannot be broken),

3. What is Jesus asking them?

John 10:36 NKJV
do you say of Him whom the Father sanctified and sent into the world, 'You are blaspheming,' because I said, 'I am the Son of God'?

4. When should they not believe a man?

John 10:37 NKJV
If I do not do the works of My Father, do not believe Me;

5. What is Jesus addressing in this verse?

John 10:38 NKJV
but if I do, though you do not believe Me, believe the works, that you may know and believe that the Father is in Me, and I in Him."

*If they cannot believe in Him, they should at least believe in the works He does. Then they would know that He could not do those works without the Father being in Him.

6. What are the Jews again seeking to do?

John 10:39 NKJV
Therefore, they sought again to seize Him, but He escaped out of their hand.

7. Where did Jesus go?

John 10:40 NKJV
And He went away again beyond the Jordan to the place where John was baptizing at first, and there He stayed.

8. A. Did John the Baptist do any miracles?

    B. What are the believers saying?

John 10:41 NKJV
Then many came to Him and said, "John performed no sign, but all the things that John spoke about this Man were true."

9. Did any believe on Him?

John 10:42 NKJV
And many believed in Him there.

Answers:
1. The Jews did not think it was a double standard or blasphemy to be called "gods" (with a small g) in the Old Testament, but they are accusing Jesus when He calls Himself Son of God.
2. The ones' called gods were those whom the Word of God came to.
3. How can you say I blaspheme? I am the One that the Father has sanctified and sent into the world. I am greater than the ones who received the Word, I am the Word. John 1:1,14.

4. Do not believe a man when he does not the works of God.
5. He is again addressing their unbelief.
6. The Jews want to kill Jesus.
7. Jesus went beyond Jordan to the place where John the Baptist first baptized.
8. A. No, John the Baptist didn't do any miracles. B. All the things that John spoke of this man are true.
9. Yes, many believed on Him.

Outline:
- The Old Testament law described believers as gods with a little "g".
- Those who the Word of God came to were characterized as little gods.
- They are calling Jesus a blasphemer and yet holding themselves in high regard through Old Testament Scriptures.
- Jesus says that His works testify of Him.
- Let the good works of Jesus lead you to belief.
- Believe that Jesus is in the Father and the Father in Him.
- No one can seize Jesus. He consistently escapes. It isn't His time.
- Many did believe on Jesus.
- False leaders are accusers not protectors.

Thoughts to Ponder:
1. Do you know and trust your shepherd intimately? Trusting Christ is a place of peaceful resting, not anxious fretting.

2. Do you know the voice of your shepherd? The shepherd gently leads, He is not a harsh taskmaster.

3. Can you quiet yourself and feel His peace come anytime you are anxious?

Challenge: Look up a few verses that say "in" Christ. There are 106 verses to choose from in the NIV version of the Bible. Use whatever version you like. Tell me how safe you are "in" Christ.

Write a prayer and ask God to teach you how to be "in" Him. This is a place of safety that goes beyond temporal suffering and lands in the glory of God. Romans 8:18

John 11

There is no stumbling with the light of Jesus.

... he does not stumble, because he sees the light of this world. John 11:9

Day 53

1. A. Who was sick?

   B. Where did he live?

   C. Who was with him?

John 11:1 NKJV
Now a certain man was sick, Lazarus of Bethany, the town of Mary and her sister Martha.

2. A. What was Mary known for?

   B. Who was her brother?

John 11:2 NKJV
It was that Mary who anointed the Lord with fragrant oil and wiped His feet with her hair, whose brother Lazarus was sick.

3. What did the sisters do when their brother, Lazarus was sick?

John 11:3 NKJV
Therefore, the sisters sent to Him, saying, "Lord, behold, he whom You love is sick."

4. Why would Jesus tarry before answering their plea?

John 11:4 NKJV
When Jesus heard that, He said, "This sickness is not unto death, but for the glory of God, that the Son of God may be glorified through it."

5. Did Jesus love Mary, Martha, and Lazarus?

John 11:5 NKJV
Now Jesus loved Martha and her sister and Lazarus.

6. Did Jesus come right away?

John 11:6 NKJV
So, when He heard that he was sick, He stayed two more days in the place where He was.

7. After 2 days, what did Jesus say?

John 11:7 NKJV
Then after this He said to the disciples, "Let us go to Judea again."

8. What did His disciples say? /

John 11:8 NKJV
The disciples said to Him, "Rabbi, lately the Jews sought to stone You, and are You going there again?"

9. What did Jesus's answer mean?

John 11:9 NKJV
Jesus answered, "Are there not twelve hours in the day? If anyone walks in the day, he does not stumble, because he sees the light of this world.

10. Can a man see where he is going if he walks without Jesus? (see John 1:9; 3:19; 5:35; 12:35,36,46)

John 11:10 NKJV
But if one walks in the night, he stumbles, because the light is not in him."

Answers:
1. A. Lazarus was sick. B. He lived in Bethany C. Mary and Martha his sisters were with him.
2. A. The one who anointed the Lord with ointment and wiped His feet with her hair. B. Mary's brother was Lazarus.
3. The sisters called for Jesus when Lazarus got sick.
4. Jesus tarried for the glory of God.
5. Jesus loved Mary, Martha, and Lazarus.
6. No, Jesus didn't come right away, He stayed where He was for two days.
7. Jesus said, let us go into Judea again.
8. Why are you going to Judea, they want to kill you there?
9. Jesus could see where He was going because He was walking in the light.
10. No, walking in darkness causes stumbling.

Outline:
- Lazarus was sick.
- Mary, Martha, and Lazarus were special friends that always opened their home to Jesus.
- Mary was the one who had anointed Jesus's feet and sat at the feet of Jesus to be taught.
- Some sicknesses are for the glory of God.
- Jesus prolonged his arrival until Lazarus was dead and buried.
- Jesus and the disciples were going to have to go through Judea where they wanted to stone Jesus.
- Jesus answers the disciples by telling them He is walking in the light and will not stumble.

Thoughts to Ponder:
1. Can you be safe for yourself and not fret when things don't go the way you want them to?

2. Can you move the confusing (dark) things out of your mind and be grateful for the good things?

3. Is there a situation in your life where Jesus has tarried and not answered?

Challenges: Can you have faith when you don't understand the thoughts or plans of the Lord? Write Isaiah 55:8.

Write a prayer for a heart of faith to believe God even when things look impossible.

Day 54

Jesus speaks plainly.

And I am glad for your sakes that I was not there, that you may believe. John 11:15

1. Did Jesus know that Lazarus was dead?

John 11:11 NKJV
These things He said, and after that He said to them, "Our friend Lazarus sleeps, but I go that I may wake him up."

2. Did the disciples understand that he was dead?

John 11:12 NKJV
Then His disciples said, "Lord, if he sleeps, he will get well."

3. What did the disciples think Jesus was saying?

John 11:13 NKJV
However, Jesus spoke of his death, but they thought that He was speaking about taking rest in sleep.

4. What did Jesus say plainly to the disciples?

John 11:14 NKJV
Then Jesus said to them plainly, "Lazarus is dead.

5. What was the purpose of Lazarus' death?

John 11:15 NKJV

And I am glad for your sakes that I was not there, that you may believe. Nevertheless, let us go to him."

6. Thomas the twin has trouble with unbelief (see John 20:24-31) Possibly Thomas thinks Jesus will be killed in Judea and he has heard Lazarus is dead, so what does he then say?

John 11:16 NKJV
Then Thomas, who is called the Twin, said to his fellow disciples, "Let us also go, that we may die with Him."

7. When Jesus arrived how long had Lazarus been in the grave?

John 11:17 NKJV
So, when Jesus came, He found that he had already been in the tomb four days.

8. Where was Bethany?

John 11:18 NKJV
Now Bethany was near Jerusalem, about two miles away.

9. Who were with Mary and Martha?

John 11:19 NKJV
And many of the Jews had joined the women around Martha and Mary, to comfort them concerning their brother.

Answers:
1. Yes, Jesus knows Lazarus is dead.
2. No, the disciples do not know Lazarus is dead.
3. The disciples' thought Jesus was saying that Lazarus was just resting.
4. Jesus plainly said, Lazarus is dead.
5. The purpose of Lazarus's death is so others may believe.
6. Thomas thinks the religious leaders have the power to kill Jesus, so he says, let us go, that we may die with Him.
7. Lazarus had been dead for 4 days by the time Jesus and the disciples arrived.
8. Bethany is approximately 2 miles from Jerusalem.
9. Many other Jews were with Mary and Martha.

Outline:
- Lazarus is dead.
- The disciples are confused about the situation of Lazarus being asleep.

- Jesus often spoke in parables, but finally He spoke with clarity. Lazarus is dead.
- There is a purpose in Lazarus's death. It was for others to believe.
- To travel to get to Lazarus, the disciples had to go through Jerusalem to get to Bethany.
- Lazarus had been dead 4 days.
- Others from the community were there to comfort Mary and Martha, Lazarus's sisters.

Thoughts to Ponder:

1. Can you wait patiently during difficulties and praise God even when things look bad?

2. Can you see beyond the temporal earthly situations in your life and set your affections on things above? Colossians 3:2; Matthew 6:33

3. Do you connect emotionally to negative circumstances? What kind of circumstances cause you the most stress?

Challenge: Give God an impossible situation in your life that makes you feel powerless. Feel your emotion and release it quickly. Feel it again and validate it without attaching to the situation but attach to God and His peace. Learn to find a safe internal space for yourself.

Write out this verse and turn it into a prayer for something impossible in your life: Matthew 19:26

Day 55

Resurrection Life

Jesus said to her, "<u>I am the resurrection and the life.</u>" John 11:25

1. Who went and met Jesus?

John 11:20 NKJV
Now Martha, as soon as she heard that Jesus was coming, went and met Him, but Mary was sitting in the house.

2. What did Martha say to Jesus?

John 11:21 NKJV
Now Martha said to Jesus, "Lord, if You had been here, my brother would not have died.

3. Does Martha believe in Jesus?

John 11:22 NKJV
But even now I know that whatever You ask of God, God will give You."

4. What did Jesus say to her?

John 11:23 NKJV
Jesus said to her, "Your brother will rise again."

5. Did Martha think He was talking about now?

John 11:24 NKJV
Martha said to Him, "I know that he will rise again in the resurrection at the last day."

6. A. Who is the resurrection?

B. What's the requirement for resurrection?

John 11:25 NKJV
Jesus said to her, "<u>I am the resurrection and the life</u>. He who believes in Me, though he may die, he shall live.

7.   A. If we believe in Jesus, will we ever die (spiritually)?

B. What did Jesus ask Martha?

John 11:26 NKJV
And whoever lives and believes in Me shall never die. Do you believe this?"

8.   Who did Martha say Jesus was?

*Martha had revelation knowledge of Jesus being the Son of God. But she had not experienced Him as the resurrected life.
John 11:27 NKJV
She said to Him, "Yes, Lord, I believe that You are the Christ, the Son of God, who is to come into the world."

9.   A. Then what did Martha do?

B. What did she say to Mary?

John 11:28 NKJV
And when she had said these things, she went her way and secretly called Mary her sister, saying, "The Teacher has come and is calling for you."

10. How did Mary go to Jesus?

John 11:29 NKJV
As soon as she heard that, she arose quickly and came to Him.

11. Had Jesus arrived in Bethany?

John 11:30 NKJV
Now Jesus had not yet come into the town but was in the place where Martha met Him.

12. Where did the Jews with Mary think she was going?

John 11:31 NKJV
Then the Jews who were with her in the house, and comforting her, when they saw that Mary rose up quickly and went out, followed her, saying, "She is going to the tomb to weep there."

Answers:
1. Martha went to meet Jesus.
2. Martha tells Jesus if He had been there that her brother would not have died.
3. Martha knows that Jesus will receive whatever He asks from the Father.
4. Jesus encourages Martha by saying your brother will rise again.
5. No, Martha did not think Jesus was talking about now, she thought He meant the final resurrection.
6. A. Jesus, is the resurrection. B. We must believe to have resurrection life.
7. A. We will never die if we believe in Jesus. B. Jesus asked Martha if she believed.
8. Martha knew Jesus as the Son of God.
9. A. Next, Martha went and got Mary, her sister. B. Martha refers to Jesus as Master and tells Mary that He is calling for her.
10. Mary went to Jesus quickly.
11. Martha had met Jesus, and He was not yet in Bethany.
12. When Mary left the house quickly, others thought she was going to the tomb to weep.

Outline:
- Martha meets Jesus.
- Martha is regretting that Jesus had not been there to save Lazarus.
- Martha knows Jesus will get whatever He asks from the Father.
- Martha believed in the resurrection for a later time.
- Jesus is the resurrection.
- We will not die if we believe in Jesus.
- Martha knew Jesus as the Son of God.
- Jesus calls for Mary and Martha goes to get her.
- Mary goes quickly to Jesus.
- Others didn't know she was meeting Jesus, they thought she was going to the tomb to weep.

Thoughts to Ponder:
1. Ponder what it would feel like to know the Father so well, that we would feel He always hears and answers us.

2. Do you know the heart of your Father is to always heal?

3. Do you experience Jesus as your friend to call in time of need?

Challenge: Practice thinking an emotion, not just feeling it. Yield the feeling to the Lord and ask for grace to change the things you can and accept the things you cannot change.

Write a prayer and ask God to give you the experience of knowing Jesus as the resurrection life.

Book of John

Day 56

Jesus calls the dead.

"Lazarus, come forth!" John 11:43

1. What did Mary say to Jesus?

John 11:32 NKJV
Then, when Mary came where Jesus was, and saw Him, she fell down at His feet, saying to Him, "Lord, if You had been here, my brother would not have died."

2. Why did Jesus's spirit groan and become troubled?

John 11:33 NKJV
Therefore, when Jesus saw her weeping, and the Jews who came with her weeping, He groaned in the spirit and was troubled.

3. What did Jesus ask her?

John 11:34 NKJV
And He said, "Where have you laid him?" They said to Him, "Lord, come and see."

4. What did Jesus do?

John 11:35 NKJV
Jesus wept.

5. What did the Jews say?

John 11:36 NKJV
Then the Jews said, "See how He loved him!"

6. What were the people saying?

John 11:37 NKJV
And some of them said, "Could not this Man, who opened the eyes of the blind, also have kept this man from dying?"

7. A. What was Jesus's reaction?

   B. Where was the tomb?

John 11:38 NKJV
Then Jesus, again groaning in Himself, came to the tomb. It was a cave, and a stone lay against it.

8. A. What was Jesus's instructions at the tomb?

   B. Why was Martha shocked at this request?

John 11:39 NKJV
Jesus said, "Take away the stone." Martha, the sister of him who was dead, said to Him, "Lord, by this time there is a stench, for he has been dead four days."

9. What does it take to see the glory of God?

John 11:40 NKJV
Jesus said to her, "Did I not say to you that if you would believe you would see the <u>glory of God</u>?"

10. A. Did they take away the stone?

    B. Who did Jesus talk to next?

    C. Does the Father always hear Jesus?

John 11:41 NKJV
Then they took away the stone from the place where the dead man was lying. And Jesus lifted up His eyes and said, "Father, I thank You that You have heard Me.

Book of John

11. Why is Jesus speaking out loud to the Father?

John 11:42 NKJV
And I know that You always hear Me, but because of the people who are standing by I said this, that they may believe that You sent Me."

12. How does Jesus' call Lazarus from the grave?

John 11:43 NKJV
Now when He had said these things, He cried with a loud voice, "Lazarus, come forth!"

13. A. What did Lazarus look like when he came out of the grave?

B. What did Jesus' command?

John 11:44 NKJV
And he who had died came out bound hand and foot with graveclothes, and his face was wrapped with a cloth. Jesus said to them, "Loose him, and let him go."

Answers:

1. Mary's words to Jesus were Lord, if You had been here, my brother had not died.
2. Maybe Jesus wept because of Mary's weeping. Maybe her sadness made Him sad.
3. Jesus asked where is Lazarus?
4. Jesus wept.
5. The Jews say, behold how He loved him.
6. The Jews couldn't figure it out. If Jesus loved him enough to cry over him then couldn't He have saved Lazarus?
7. A. Jesus reacted with groaning. B. The tomb was in a cave.
8. A. Jesus instructed them to take the stone away. B. Martha was shocked because Lazarus would stink by now.
9. It takes belief to see the glory of God.
10. A. Yes, the people listened to Jesus and took away the stone. B. Jesus looks up and speaks to the Father. C. Yes, the Father always hears Jesus.
11. Jesus spoke audibly to the Father so the people may believe.
12. Jesus called Lazarus by crying out with a loud voice.
13. A. Lazarus was bound hand and foot with grave clothes and his face was bound with a napkin. B. Jesus commanded the people to loosen Lazarus.

Outline:

- Mary felt like all was lost because Jesus hadn't been there.

- Jesus showed compassion through His tears.
- Jesus loved Lazarus and his sisters.
- Jesus didn't come sooner to save Lazarus, He wanted to show the power of God that the people may believe in Him as the *resurrection*.
- Jesus required Martha to go against her instincts and against the reality of her brother's death and obey.
- It takes belief to see the glory of God.
- Jesus prays openly.
- Jesus speaks to the dead with authority.
- We need to help each other to remove the stench of the grave clothes of death and sin off us so we may live more freely with Christ.

Thoughts to Ponder:
1. What stench of the past is on you that you need to get off?

2. Guilt, shame and self-condemnation is false humility. So, it's pride. Only solution is to repent your way out of it. Lord, forgive me....

3. Do you believe that Jesus is the resurrection?

Challenge: Detach from things that make you suffer. Do this by breathing and pushing the stress outside of yourself and not identifying with it. Name a person, place, or circumstance you want to detach from and practice doing this several times a day until it has no power of over anymore.

Book of John

Write a prayer for resurrection life in an area of your life that feels dead.

Angie Meadows

Day 57

Miracles increase Belief.

Many...had seen the things Jesus did, (and) believed in Him. John 11:45

1. What did this miracle do in the hearts of the people?

John 11:45 NKJV
Then many of the Jews who had come to Mary, and had seen the things Jesus did, believed in Him.

2. Who did some of them tattle to?

John 11:46 NKJV
But some of them went away to the Pharisees and told them the things Jesus did.

3. Why were the Pharisees worried?

John 11:47 NKJV
Then the chief priests and the Pharisees gathered a council and said, "What shall we do? For this Man works many signs.

4. Why were the miracles such a problem?

John 11:48 NKJV
If we let Him alone like this, everyone will believe in Him, and the Romans will come and take away both our place and nation."

5. What did the high priest say?

*Their fears were unfounded.

Book of John

John 11:49 NKJV
And one of them, Caiaphas, being high priest that year, said to them, "You know nothing at all,

6. Caiaphas was speaking prophecy about what?

John 11:50 NKJV
nor do you consider that it is expedient for us that one man should die for the people, and not that the whole nation should perish."

7. Was this thought from Caiaphas?

John 11:51 NKJV
Now this he did not say on his own authority; but being high priest that year he prophesied that Jesus would die for the nation,

8. What other purpose was Jesus to die for?

*This was speaking of the Gentiles being saved also.
John 11:52 NKJV
and not for that nation only, but also that He would gather together in one the children of God who were scattered abroad.

9. From that day forth the Pharisees talked about what?

John 11:53 NKJV
Then, from that day on, they plotted to put Him to death.

10. A. Was Jesus able to walk openly now?

    B. What did He do in Ephraim?

John 11:54 NKJV
Therefore, Jesus no longer walked openly among the Jews, but went from there into the country near the wilderness, to a city called Ephraim, and there remained with His disciples.

11. What time of year was it?

John 11:55 NKJV
And the Passover of the Jews was near, and many went from the country up to Jerusalem before the Passover, to purify themselves.

12. What did the Pharisees ask each other?

John 11:56 NKJV
Then they sought Jesus, and spoke among themselves as they stood in the temple, "What do you think-that He will not come to the feast?"

13. A. What was the command of the high priests and Pharisees?

    B. Why did they want to know?

John 11:57 NKJV
Now both the chief priests and the Pharisees had given a command, that if anyone knew where He was, he should report it, that they might seize Him.

Answers:
1. When Lazarus was raised from the dead, the people believed.
2. Some tattled to the Pharisees.
3. They didn't know what to do with someone doing all these miracles.
4. They were worried people would believe in Jesus and they would lose their jobs and political power.
5. The high priest said you know nothing at all.
6. The high priest prophesied about Jesus's death.
7. Caiaphas's prophecy came from being a high priest.
8. Jesus died so He could gather the children of God that were scattered abroad.
9. The Pharisees talked about how to put Jesus to death.
10. A. No, Jesus couldn't walk openly now. B. Jesus remained with His disciples.
11. The time of year was the Passover.
12. Pharisees wondered and said do you think Jesus will come to the feast?
13. A. If anyone knows where He is, He is to tell them. B. So they could capture and kill Him.

Outline:
- Miracles help people believe.
- Even with miracles, there will always be backstabbers and people trying to skew your motives.

- The miracles caused the Pharisees to want to question how they should exert their power.
- A thirst for political power can cause selfish people to make wrong decisions.
- The high priest was able to prophesy things that even he didn't understand.
- Children of God are Jews and Gentiles.
- The Pharisees sought to kill Jesus and He could no longer walk openly.
- Passover is a feast in memory of the time in Egypt during the plague of the death of the firstborn where the Israelites put the blood of a lamb over their doorposts and the death angel passed by them.
- The Pharisees were jealous and were planning on using their power to kill Jesus.

Thoughts to Ponder:

1. What do you think you should do in a situation where others are jealous of you?

2. Can you recognize when you are jealous of others?

3. How could you correct yourself when you are envious or jealous of others?

Challenge: Pray for the ones in authority over you to have pure hearts and to be true shepherds of their people.

Write a prayer that you would be able to come along side of leaders and genuinely nurture and support them without jealousy.

Book of John

John 12
Day 58

Worship is fragrance.

...the house was filled with the fragrance of the oil. John 12:3

1. A. Where was Jesus?

   B. What had happened there?

John 12:1 NKJV
Then, six days before the Passover, Jesus came to Bethany, where Lazarus was who had been dead, whom He had raised from the dead.

2. A. What was Jesus doing in Bethany?

   B. Who served Him?

   C. Who was with Him?

John 12:2 NKJV

There they made Him a supper; and Martha served, but Lazarus was one of those who sat at the table with Him.

3. What did Mary do?

John 12:3 NKJV
Then Mary took a pound of very costly oil of spikenard, anointed the feet of Jesus, and wiped His feet with her hair. And the house was filled with the fragrance of the oil.

4. Who was Judas?

John 12:4 NKJV
But one of His disciples, Judas Iscariot, Simon's son, who would betray Him, said,

5. What was the heart condition of Judas?

John 12:5 NKJV
"Why was this fragrant oil not sold for three hundred denarii and given to the poor?"

6. Judas was what kind of man?

*Our heart conditions that are impure must be identified and corrected or they will be a trap to rob us of our position in Christ.
John 12:6 NKJV
This he said, not that he cared for the poor, but because he was a thief, and had the money box; and he used to take what was put in it.

7. What was Jesus referring to?

* Intense worship is sacrificial.
John 12:7 NKJV
But Jesus said, "Let her alone; she has kept this for the day of My burial.

8. Did His disciples understand this?

John 12:8 NKJV

For the poor you have with you always, but Me you do not have always."

9. Why did the people come?

John 12:9 NKJV
Now a great many of the Jews knew that He was there; and they came, not for Jesus' sake only, but that they might also see Lazarus, whom He had raised from the dead.

10. What did the chief priest want to do?

John 12:10 NKJV
But the chief priests plotted to put Lazarus to death also,

11. Why would they want to put Lazarus to death?

John 12:11 NKJV
because on account of him many of the Jews went away and believed in Jesus.

12. Were the people following Jesus?

John 12:12 NKJV
The next day a great multitude that had come to the feast, when they heard that Jesus was coming to Jerusalem,

Answers:
1. A. Jesus was in Bethany. B. Lazarus was risen from the dead.
2. A. Jesus was eating supper. B. Martha served Jesus. C. Lazarus was with Jesus.
3. She took one pound of spikenard and anointed Jesus's feet and wiped them with her hair.
4. Judas was the Son of Simon and one of the disciples of Jesus. He was the one that would betray Jesus.
5. Judas's heart condition was greed.
6. Judas was a thief.
7. Jesus was referring to His death.
8. No, the disciples didn't understand that Jesus was going to die.
9. The people came because of curiosity and to see someone raised from the dead.
10. The chief priest wanted to put Lazarus to death.
11. The Pharisees wanted to protect their own selfish interest. He drew attention to Jesus. He was a reminder of Jesus's power.
12. Yes, many people came.

Outline:
- Lazarus is now risen from the dead.
- Jesus fellowshipped with Mary, Martha, and Lazarus.
- Mary anointed Jesus's feet.
- A heart condition of greed could lead to the behavior of being a thief and later to betrayal and self-destruction.
- Mary anointed Jesus for His death and burial.
- People may come to see Jesus from curiosity.
- Pharisees plotted to kill Lazarus and Jesus.

Thoughts to Ponder:
1. Why might others put missionaries/Christians to death today?

2. Would you die for your belief in Christ?

3. Would you live for Christ every day?

Challenge: Examine your own heart. What is the one character flaw that might trip you up?

Write a prayer ask the Lord for a faith bigger than your fears.

Book of John

Day 59

Jesus saves.

"Hosanna! 'Blessed is He who comes in the name of the LORD!' John 12:13

1. What were the people doing?

*Hosanna is Aramaic for "God save" or "God help". This is known as the triumphal entry.
John 12:13 NKJV
took branches of palm trees and went out to meet Him and cried out: "Hosanna! 'Blessed is He who comes in the name of the LORD!' The King of Israel!"

2. Why was it important for Him to be on a young ass?

* Zech. 9:9 "... thy King cometh unto thee: he is just, and having salvation; lowly, and riding upon an ass, and upon a colt the foal of an ass."
John 12:14 NKJV
Then Jesus, when He had found a young donkey, sat on it as it is written:

3. Would you expect your King to be on a lowly donkey?

John 12:15 NKJV
"Fear not, daughter of Zion; Behold, your King is coming, Sitting on a donkey's colt."

4. Did the disciples understand?

*But after the resurrection then they remembered the prophecies about him.
John 12:16 NKJV
His disciples did not understand these things at first; but when Jesus was glorified, then they remembered that these things were written about Him and that they had done these things to Him.

5. Who bore record of Lazarus's resurrection?

John 12:17 NKJV
Therefore, the people, who were with Him when He called Lazarus out of his tomb and raised him from the dead, bore witness.

6. Why did the multitudes gather to Him?

John 12:18 NKJV
For this reason, the people also met Him, because they heard that He had done this sign.

7. Were the Pharisees jealous?

John 12:19 NKJV
The Pharisees therefore said among themselves, "You see that you are accomplishing nothing. Look, the world has gone after Him!"

8. Who worshipped with them at the Passover?

John 12:20 NKJV
Now there were certain Greeks among those who came up to worship at the feast.

9. Who came to Phillip inquiring to see Jesus?

John 12:21 NKJV
Then they came to Philip, who was from Bethsaida of Galilee, and asked him, saying, "Sir, we wish to see Jesus."

10. A. Who did Phillip tell? (John 1:40-42)

    B. What was Andrew good at doing?

John 12:22 NKJV

Philip came and told Andrew, and in turn Andrew and Philip told Jesus.

Answers:
1. The people are worshipping.
2. The donkey was fulfillment of prophecy.
3. No, you would expect a King to come with horses and an army.
4. No, the disciples did not understand.
5. The people who were with Him at Lazarus's grave bore witness of the power of Jesus to be the resurrection.
6. The multitudes gathered to Jesus because they had heard He had done a great miracle.
7. Yes, the people were all going after Jesus and not them. So, the Pharisees were afraid of losing their influence.
8. The Greeks worshipped with the Jews at Passover.
9. The Greeks wanted to meet Jesus.
10. A. Philip told Andrew. B. Andrew took the people to Jesus.

Outline:
- The people worshipped Jesus.
- The donkey was fulfillment of Old Testament prophecy.
- The disciples consistently struggle to understand what is happening.
- Jesus is becoming known for His miracles and resurrection power.
- Many wanted to see Jesus. Even the Greeks wanted to meet Him.
- The Pharisees are consistently afraid of losing their influence and power.
- The disciple Andrew was consistently taking people to Jesus.

Thoughts to Ponder:
1. Who do you know that consistently takes others to Jesus?

2. Who are those that you need to avoid or hide from, so they don't mock your ministry and walk with Jesus?

3. Do you follow Jesus out of curiosity or from a heart of love?

Challenge: Keep on the lookout for fulfillment of Old Testament prophecies of Jesus as the Messiah.

Write a prayer and ask the Father to enlighten your spiritual eyes to see Jesus as your source of spiritual resurrection and renewal.

Book of John

Day 60

Death to self=Life in Christ

...but if it dies, it produces much grain. John 12:24

1. What does this mean?

John 12:23 NKJV
But Jesus answered them, saying, "The hour has come that the Son of Man should be glorified.

2. What happens to corn of wheat in the ground?

John 12:24 NKJV
Most assuredly, I say to you, unless a grain of wheat falls into the ground and dies, it remains alone; but if it dies, it produces much grain.

3. What does Jesus want us to do?

John 12:25 NKJV
He who loves his life will lose it, and he who hates his life in this world will keep it for eternal life.

4. A. What does He want us to do?

B. What blessing will we receive if we do this?

John 12:26 NKJV
If anyone serves Me, let him follow Me; and where I am, there My servant will be also. If anyone serves Me, him My Father will honor.

5. A. Is Jesus troubled?

B. Why is He not saved from this hour?

John 12:27 NKJV
"Now my soul is troubled, and what shall I say? 'Father, save Me from this hour'? But for this purpose, I came to this hour.

6. A. Does Christ glorify God?

B. What does God's voice say?

C. Glorify what?

John 12:28 NKJV
Father, glorify Your name." Then a voice came from heaven, saying, "I have both glorified it and will glorify it again."

7. A. Did the people hear the voice of God?

B. Did it sound like our voice?

*Maybe those who believed had open spiritual ears and others with unbelief heard thunder were spiritually deaf.
John 12:29 NKJV
Therefore, the people who stood by and heard it said that it had thundered. Others said, "An angel has spoken to Him."

8. A. Did Jesus need to hear God's voice out loud?

B. But who did need to hear God's voice?

John 12:30 NKJV

Jesus answered and said, "This voice did not come because of Me, but for your sake.

9. Who was the prince of this world to be judged? (John 14:30; 16:11)

John 12:31 NKJV
Now is the judgment of this world; now the ruler of this world will be cast out.

10. What was one of the purposes of Christ on the cross?

John 12:32 NKJV
And I, if I am lifted up from the earth, will draw all peoples to Myself."

11. What does lifted from the earth in verse 32 mean?

John 12:33 NKJV
This He said, signifying by what death He would die.

12. A. Does Christ abide forever?

B. Who is questioning Jesus?

*They just heard the voice of God speak to Him and they still don't believe Him.
John 12:34 NKJV
The people answered Him, "We have heard from the law that the Christ remains forever; and how can You say, 'The Son of Man must be lifted up'? Who is this Son of Man?"

13. If Christ abides forever, why does darkness come?

*The secret is in the next study in the next verse.
John 12:35 NKJV
Then Jesus said to them, "A little while longer the light is with you. Walk while you have the light, lest darkness overtake you; he who walks in darkness does not know where he is going.

Answers:
1. Son of man will be glorified by death on the cross.
2. A corn of wheat dies, decomposes, and then brings new blade/new life and bears much fruit.
3. Jesus wants us to lay down our will, desires, and feelings and ask for His will. We are to love Him and obey Him and not to follow this world.
4. Jesus tells His disciples to follow Him and serve Him. B. If we do this, we will be honored by the Father.
5. A. Yes, Jesus is troubled. B. Jesus is not saved from this hour because for this reason He came into the world.
6. A. Yes, Christ always glorifies God the Father. B. I have both glorified it and will glorify it again. C. Jesus will glorify the Father's name.
7. A. Yes, the people heard the voice of God. B. No, it was loud like thunder.
8. A. No, Jesus does not need to hear the voice of God out loud. B. Those that were with Him needed to hear/sense/feel the voice of God.
9. Satan is the prince of this world.
10. One of the purposes of the cross was to draw all men unto Him.
11. So, the people would know how He was to die.
12. A. Yes, Christ abides forever. B. The people are questioning Jesus.
13. Like the sun, Christ is not always visible, but He is always there.

Outline:
- Jesus glorified the Father by laying down His life.
- As a kernel of wheat must die before it can produce an abundant harvest, so must we die to our flesh to live in the Spirit.
- Laying down my own will and seeking God for His will brings me freedom.
- Even Jesus was troubled in His spirit, so if we are troubled, we are to keep trusting and moving forward.
- Sensing, feeling, and hearing the voice of God in our spirit is a sign of maturity.
- If I indulge my exaggerated emotions or my soulish side, I will be joining forces with the prince of this world.
- Christ lives and abides forever.
- Learn to move the darkness and embrace the light.

Thoughts to Ponder:
1. Do you follow Jesus because of a love in your heart for Him as your Master and Teacher?

2. Does it feel weird to refer to Jesus as your Master, Savior, or Messiah?

3. Is there any area of your life where you are embracing your insecurity more than you are trusting the Lord

Challenge: If you cannot sing, your spirit may be bound with deceitfulness and the cares of the world. (Mark 4:19) This heart posture will rob you of the fruit. Ask the Lord to set you free to sing, worship and enjoy your days.

Write a prayer ask God to reveal any hidden division in your heart that hinders your walk with Him.

Day 61

God praises me for my belief.

...for they loved the praise of men more than the praise of God. John 12:43

1. A. What's the key word Jesus is speaking to them?

   B. What's the secret to walking out of darkness into the light?

John 12:36 NKJV
While you have the light, <u>believe in the light</u>, that you may become sons of light." These things Jesus spoke, and departed, and was hidden from them.

2. A. Did they believe Him?

   B. What had He done for them to believe?

   *It is vital that when we start to forget God that we remember all the miracles and answered prayers he has done for us.

John 12:37 NKJV
But although He had done so many signs before them, they did not believe in Him,

3. A. Does all the Bible's prophecy have to be fulfilled?

John 12:38 NKJV
that the word of Isaiah the prophet might be fulfilled, which he spoke: "Lord, who has believed our report? And to whom has the arm of the LORD been revealed?"

4. Was it prophesied that they would believe?

Book of John

John 12:39 NKJV
Therefore, they could not believe, because Isaiah said again:

5. A. Whose hearts would be hardened and eyes blinded?

   B. What are the two promises to the ones who believed?

*Conversion – A change in direction or a new walk with God.
*Healing – A change in health: mental, emotional, physical, relational, and financial.
John 12:40 NKJV
"He has blinded their eyes and hardened their hearts, lest they should see with their eyes, lest they should understand with their hearts and turn, so that I should heal them."

6. Did Isaiah see the coming of Jesus?

John 12:41 NKJV
These things Isaiah said when he saw His glory and spoke of Him.

7. A. Did some believe?

   B. Why didn't they confess Christ?

John 12:42 NKJV
Nevertheless, even among the rulers many believed in Him, but because of the Pharisees they did not confess Him, lest they should be put out of the synagogue.

8. Why couldn't they confess Christ?

John 12:43 NKJV
for they loved the praise of men more than the praise of God.

Answers:
1. A. The key word is "BELIEVE". B. The secret to moving the darkness is to believe in the light and the light is Jesus Christ.
2. A. No, the people did not believe in Jesus. B. Jesus had done many miracles among them.
3. A. Yes, when Bible prophesies are fulfilled, this increases our belief.
4. No, it was prophesied that they would not believe.
5. A. Those with unbelief would develop hardened the heart. B. The promise was conversion and healing.
6. Yes, the prophet Isaiah saw the coming of the Lord Jesus.
7. A. Yes, some believed. B. Some did not confess Christ because of the fear of man; they did not want to be put out of the synagogue.
8. Some loved the praise of men, more than they loved the praise of God.

Outline:
- The darkness is characterized by confusion and shrinking back because of the fear of man and fear of being ostracized.
- A hardened heart is formed from unbelief.
- The light of Jesus Christ will make you bold through your belief.
- Maturity cares more about walking with Christ than having the approval of people.
- Prophecies are to strengthen our belief.

Thoughts to Ponder:
1. Rehearse answered prayers in your life in this space.

2. Have you ever had a word prophesied or spoken over your life? If not, ask for one in this space.

3. Outline one personal goal for maturity in each area of life: physical, mental, emotional, spiritual, relational, or financial.

Physical self-care goal:

Emotional maturity goal:

Spiritual maturity goal:

Relational maturity goal:

Financial maturity goal:

Challenge: Is there an area of your life with a selfish bent that you need to confess?

Write a prayer and confess your unbelief (exhibited by anxiety, fear, stress, fretting). Now pray that God would give you the gift of faith to be an overcomer of Romans 12:21?

Angie Meadows

Day 62

Christ saves.

And I know that His (Father's) command is everlasting life.
John 12:50

1. When you believe in Christ, you also believe what?

John 12:44 NKJV
Then Jesus cried out and said, "He who believes in Me, believes not in Me but in Him who sent Me.

2. If we truly can see Christ, what else is natural for us to see?

John 12:45 NKJV
And he who sees Me sees Him who sent Me.

3. A. Belief brings what?

   B. Unbelief brings what?

John 12:46 NKJV
I have come as a light into the world, that whoever believes in Me should not abide in darkness.

4. Was Christ here at this time to judge us?

John 12:47 NKJV
And if anyone hears My words and does not believe, I do not judge him; for I did not come to judge the world but to save the world.

5. Who/what will judge in the last day?

John 12:48 NKJV
He who rejects Me, and does not receive My words, has that which judges him - the word that I have spoken will judge him in the last day.

6. Was Jesus here for personal gain or to puff himself up?

*These are signs of a false prophet.
John 12:49 NKJV
For I have not spoken on My own authority; but the Father who sent Me gave Me a command, what I should say and what I should speak.

7. What brings everlasting life?

John 12:50 NKJV
And I know that His command is everlasting life. Therefore, whatever I speak, just as the Father has told Me, so I speak."

Answers:
1. A belief in Christ is a belief in the Father which sent Him.
2. It is natural for us to find God when we find Christ.
3. A. Belief brings light. B. Unbelief brings darkness.
4. No, Christ didn't come to judge us but to save us.
5. The word that Christ has spoken will judge us in the last day.
6. No, Jesus was here to glorify God.
7. The commandment of God that God spoke to Christ brings everlasting life.

Outline:
- Jesus and the Father are one.
- If we find Jesus, we will find the Father.
- Belief stops confusion and brings clarity.
- To be Christ-like is to stop judging yourself and others.
- Walking in belief and light will bring glory to God.
- Jesus's commandments bring everlasting life.

Thoughts to Ponder:
1. What is in your heart that feels like life?

2. What is in your heart feels like death?

3. Do you have spiritual/feeling discernment where you can listen to your body and feel if it is peaceful or anxious?

Challenge: Listen to your body today. Sense when your jaw tightens, or your shoulders lift with tension. Do you pick up environmental stress around yourself?

Can you obtain peace and rule your own spirit and deflect stressful situations?

Write a prayer by taking Proverbs 25:28 and turning it into a prayer. Ask God to help you rule your own spirit.

John 13

A divided heart leads to betrayal.

...the devil having already put it into the heart.... to betray Him, John 13:2

Day 63

1. A. What is so significant about this day being the Passover time?

   B. Did Jesus know what was going to happen to Him?

   C. Where was He going?

   D. Why is He going to the cross?

John 13:1 NKJV
Now before the Feast of the Passover, when Jesus knew that His hour had come that He should depart from this world to the Father, having loved His own who were in the world, He loved them to the end.

2. A. Why would the devil be allowed to enter and control Judas?

B. What was his heart condition like from John12:4-6?

C. Can we walk three years with Jesus and see all His miracles and still indulge an evil heart?

John 13:2 NKJV
And supper being ended, the devil having already put it into the heart of Judas Iscariot, Simon's son, to betray Him,

3. Why was Jesus so confident?

Do you know who you are in Christ? (Application)

John 13:3 NKJV
Jesus, knowing that the Father had given all things into His hands, and that He had come from God and was going to God,

4. Why did He remove His outer garment?

John 13:4 NKJV
rose from supper and laid aside His garments, took a towel and girded Himself.

5. Foot washing was a task for the lowliest slave. Christ did this for what reason?

John 13:5 NKJV
After that, He poured water into a basin and began to wash the disciples' feet, and to wipe them with the towel with which He was girded.

6. Do we sometimes question God's will?

John 13:6 NKJV
Then He came to Simon Peter. And Peter said to Him, "Lord, are You washing my feet?"

7. Do we always know ahead of time what Christ is doing in our lives?

John 13:7 NKJV
Jesus answered and said to him, "What I am doing you do not understand now, but you will know after this."

8. Did Peter want Christ at His feet in lowly servanthood?

*Peter didn't understand.
John 13:8 NKJV
Peter said to Him, "You shall never wash my feet!" Jesus answered him, "If I do not wash you, you have no part with Me."

9. Why do you think Peter said this?

John 13:9 Simon Peter said to him, "Lord, not my feet only, but also my hands and my head!"

10. How is this washing symbolic of daily repentance?

*This is symbolic of frequent repentance and need for a daily walk with Christ. It is not a complete re-salvation.
John 13:10 NKJV
Jesus said to him, "He who is bathed needs only to wash his feet, but is completely clean; and you are clean, but not all of you."

11. A. Did Jesus know that this was not a true washing for one of them?

    B. Who was it that had truly rejected this foot washing in his heart?

John 13:11 NKJV
For He knew who would betray Him; therefore, He said, "You are not all clean."

Answers:
1. A. Jesus is the sacrificial lamb. B. Yes, Jesus knew He was the lamb of God. C. Jesus was going to the Father. D. It is because He loves us.
2. A. It is because his heart wasn't devoted to righteousness. B. Judas's heart condition was greed, lying and selfishness. Greed for money – he wasn't concerned for the poor. Lying – he lied to Christ. Self-interest – he wanted the money for himself. C. Yes if we fail to renounce and turn from our sin.
3. Jesus was confident because He knew who He was and where He came from.
4. The outer garment was removed for working or sleeping.
5. Jesus did this as an example of His servanthood to us and as an example of our type of servant-leadership towards others.
6. Yes, when we don't understand.
7. No, we are to trust and walk by faith.
8. No, he thought a lot of Christ's dignity. He knew that Jesus was the Messiah.
9. Peter jumps ditches. He can be impulsive and go to the opposite extreme.
10. When we are saved, we are clean all over, but then we go out into the world and get our feet dirty, we just need our feet washed.
11. A. Yes, we must have our hearts ready for a daily foot washing. B. Judas had a divided heart and was not prepared to receive a washing (cleansing).

Outline:
- Jesus is the perfect sinless sacrifice to take away the sins of the world.
- A divided heart will cause a man to stumble and eventually betray Christ and may lead to a complete downfall.
- Knowing who we are in Christ is important for our healing and steadfast healthy faith.
- Servant leaders are Christ-like.
- Peter had his own ideas. But Christ patiently corrected him.
- Daily soul searching to keep our conscience clean is vital.
- A divided heart leads to wrong choices and self-destructive behaviors.

Thoughts to Ponder:
1. If I could discern one area in my life that was not surrendered to Christ what would it be? Would it be greed, lust, anger, selfishness, an offense, bitterness, stubbornness, or hatred. Well, no big deal, Jesus is in the business of healing emotional wounds.

2. Am I making excuses for any of my poor behaviors?

3. Do I indulge negative emotions and agree with its right to take up space in my life? Depression, anxiety, fear, stress…

Challenge: What would it look like to let Jesus wash you daily through your repentance and forgiving others every evening?

What would it look like to purpose to forgive everyone before anything ever happened?

Write a prayer and ask the Lord for a clear conscience and a freedom to experience His love and speak about Him with confidence.

Angie Meadows

Day 64

Jesus is the servant leader.

You call Me Teacher and Lord... John 13:13

1. Does Jesus want to explain His actions to us?

John 13:12 NKJV
So, when He had washed their feet, taken His garments, and sat down again, He said to them, "Do you know what I have done to you?

2. Who is Jesus?

John 13:13 NKJV
You call Me Teacher and Lord, and you say well, for so I am.

3. A. What is the sign that He is our Master and Lord?

John 13:14 NKJV
If I then, your Lord and Teacher, have washed your feet, you also ought to wash one another's feet.

4. Why did Christ wash the feet of the disciples?

John 13:15 NKJV
For I have given you an example, that you should do as I have done to you.

5. What's this verse saying?

John 13:16 NKJV
Most assuredly, I say to you, a servant is not greater than his master; nor is he who is sent greater than he who sent him.

6. What kind of things will make us happy (blessed)?

John 13:17 NKJV
If you know these things, blessed are you if you do them.

7. Why did one of His own disciples have to be the one that betrayed Him?

John 13:18 NKJV
"I do not speak concerning all of you. I know whom I have chosen; but that the Scripture may be fulfilled, 'He who eats bread with Me has lifted up his heel against Me.'

Answers:
1. Yes, but sometimes obedience comes first, then understanding.
2. Jesus is teacher and Lord (master).
3. We would willingly wash each other's feet.
4. Jesus washed the feet of the disciples to be our example.
5. Don't puff yourself up, make sure you are humble and know your place.
6. If we are a servant to others and it is reciprocated, it is very fulfilling.
7. Jesus's own disciple had to betray Him to fulfill prophetic Scriptures.

Outline:
- Obedience is doing what I know to do.
- Jesus as my teacher and master in me comes through the Holy Spirit and this fills me with his goodness and love and makes me free from the bondage of sin.
- Patiently washing the feet of others as a servant is a maturity skill. This isn't enabling or excusing laziness for another. This is a sacrificial love as an example for us to each do for one another.
- There is a balance to serving. Serving is teaching and training in life skills and character for the success of those we love.
- Sometimes, there is a Judas, and we must let go of them and turn them over to their own devices.

Thoughts to Ponder:
1. Is Jesus your Teacher, Master, and Lord?

2. Do you give Him authority over every area of your life to shape it in love and goodness?

Challenge: What would this look like in our family if we were all servants to one another?

- Would we run to do chores to surprise others?
- Would we serve another before ourselves?
- Would we care patiently for the smaller children, the sick or elderly and pets?
- Would we happily do the most menial task without being asked?

Write a prayer and ask for the strength to release a Judas and set strong boundaries in your life against their continual betrayal.

Book of John

Day 65

The beloved can ask to know secrets.

Then leaning back on Jesus' breast, he (John) said to Him, "Lord, who is it?" John 13:25

1. Jesus would speak future events to them for what reason?

John 13:19 NKJV
Now I tell you before it comes, that when it does come to pass, you may believe that I am He.

2. A. When we receive those that are sent by Christ, who are we receiving?

   B. When we receive Christ who are we really receiving?

John 13:20 NKJV
Most assuredly, I say to you, he who receives whomever I send receives Me; and he who receives Me receives Him who sent Me."

3. A. Was Jesus ever troubled in spirit?

   B. Will things happen to us that will make us troubled?

*Betrayal is troubling.
John 13:21 NKJV
When Jesus had said these things, He was <u>troubled in spirit</u>, and testified and said, "Most assuredly, I say to you, one of you will betray Me."

4. Did the disciples understand one of them was going to betray Him?

John 13:22 NKJV
Then the disciples looked at one another, perplexed about whom He spoke.

5. Who is the disciple that described himself as "the one Jesus loved"?

Application: Can we describe ourselves as the one Jesus loves?
John 13:23 NKJV
Now there was leaning on Jesus' bosom one of His disciples, whom Jesus loved.

6. Who is Simon Peter speaking to?

John 13:24 NKJV
Simon Peter therefore motioned to him to ask who it was of whom He spoke.

7. What did John do?

John 13:25 NKJV
Then, leaning back on Jesus' breast, he said to Him, "Lord, who is it?"

8. Did Jesus reveal who His betrayer was?

*Dipping and handing someone food was a sign of honor.
Jesus was honoring His enemy or maybe He was appealing to Judas's conscience/heart.
John 13:26 NKJV
Jesus answered, "It is he to whom I shall give a piece of bread when I have dipped it." And having dipped the bread, He gave it to Judas Iscariot, the son of Simon.

9. How could Satan enter Judas?

John 13:27 NKJV
Now after the piece of bread, Satan entered him. Then Jesus said to him, "What you do, do quickly."

10. Did the disciples know what Judas was going to do?

John 13:28 NKJV
But no one at the table knew for what reason He said this to him.

11. What did the disciples think Jesus was talking about?

John 13:29 NKJV
For some thought, because Judas had the money box, that Jesus had said to him, "Buy those things we need for the feast," or that he should give something to the poor.

Answers:
1. So that when the thing came to pass, they would understand that He was the Messiah.
2. A. When we receive others, we are receiving Jesus. B. When we receive Christ, we are receiving God the Father. 3. A. Yes, Jesus was troubled in His Spirit. B. Yes, Jesus had trouble, so will we.
4. Yes, it seems like the disciples understood one was going to betray Jesus.
5. John, described Himself as the one Jesus loved.
6. Peter was telling John to ask Jesus.
7. John asked Jesus, who it was that was going to betray Him.
8. Yes. Jesus dipped the bread and handed it to Judas.
9. Judas was not devoted to Christ but had a divided heart of greed.
10. No, the disciples did not know what Judas was going to do.
11. They thought it was instruction to him to go and buy something or give to the poor.

Outline:
- Prophecy was meant to increase our faith.
- Receiving those Jesus sends is receiving Him. Receiving Jesus is receiving our Father, God.
- Jesus was troubled in His spirit. How much more are we going to experience an inner turbulence during conflict or impending suffering.
- Feeling loved by Jesus will be experienced by an internal connection and an experience of closeness.
- Feeding our enemies as they are on the way out the door to betray us is a definite spiritual maturity skill that is not easy to achieve without mature faith.
- A divided heart will eventually be exposed and give Satan an opportunity to destroy us.

Thoughts to Ponder:
1. How could you honor your enemy in front of others without an ulterior motive, even knowing they were on the way out the door to betray you?

2. Are you troubled over anything today?

3. What would it take to feel loved?

Challenges: Take a small gift or token (like a cookie, a meal or small gift card) to a grumpy co-worker or neighbor.

Write a prayer and ask the Lord for a strength to believe in the face of betrayal and difficulty.

Book of John

Day 66

Jesus is Love

A new commandment I give to you.... love one another.
John 13:34

1. When is most sin committed?

John 13:30 NKJV
Having received the piece of bread, he then went out immediately. And it was night.

2. When the son of man glorified, who else is glorified?

John 13:31 NKJV
So, when he had gone out, Jesus said, "Now the Son of Man is glorified, and God is glorified in Him.

3. When Jesus glorifies the Father, what does the Father do?

John 13:32 NKJV
If God is glorified in Him, God will also glorify Him in Himself, and glorify Him immediately.

4. A. What did He call them?

   B. Could the disciples have followed Jesus?

John 13:33 NKJV
Little children, I shall be with you a little while longer. You will seek Me; and as I said to the Jews, 'Where I am going, you cannot come,' so now I say to you.

5. How is this commandment different?

*This is a pure and unselfish love to lay down your life for another. (John 15:13)
John 13:34 NKJV
A new commandment I give to you, that you love one another; as I have loved you, that you also love one another.

6. A. What were the disciples characterized by before this time? (Matthew 20:21)

   B. How can we know Jesus's true disciples?

John 13:35 NKJV
By this all will know that you are My disciples, if you have love for one another."

7. Does Simon know that Jesus is going away?

John 13:36 NKJV
Simon Peter said to Him, "Lord, where are You going?" Jesus answered him, "Where I am going you cannot follow Me now, but you shall follow Me afterward."

8. Does Peter think he can lay his life down for Jesus?

John 13:37 NKJV
Peter said to Him, "Lord, why can I not follow You now? I will lay down my life for Your sake."

9. Does Jesus know that Peter will deny him?

*Doesn't it seem like Jesus had already forgiven Peter before he even denied Him?
John 13:38 NKJV
Jesus answered him, "Will you lay down your life for My sake? Most assuredly, I say to you, the rooster shall not crow till you have denied Me three times.

Answers:
1. Most sin is committed at night under the covering of darkness.
2. When Jesus is glorified, the Father is glorified.
3. God glorifies Jesus immediately.
4. A. Jesus calls the disciples "little children". B. No, the disciples could not follow Jesus.

5. It is different because they are being called to love one another as He has loved them. And He loved them enough to lay down His life for them. He is expecting that they will lay down their lives for each other.

6.A. By envy and strife, they were wanting to be at the right and left hand of Jesus when He came into His kingdom. They wanted authority and power over each other. B. True disciples will lay down their lives for each other in the little areas of life daily.

7. Yes, but he is probably somewhat confused.

8. Yes, but he doesn't have the power of the Holy Spirit yet and his flesh is weak.

9. Yes, Jesus knew Peter would deny Him.

Outline:
- When we glorify God, He glorifies us. He likes to share His glory.
- Innocently following Jesus with a trusting heart makes me like a little child. Matthew 18:3-5
- Love is the way you are to operate in life. Love covers a multitude of sins. Proverbs 10:12
- Worldly leaders lord it over others; followers of Christ lead with servanthood and laying down their lives.
- When there is confusion sit still and ask the Lord for clarity.
- Discipleship leads to the baptism of the Holy Spirit. There is a growth process necessary with most of us called "regeneration". Romans 6:4
- There is a continual infilling of the Holy Spirit.

Thoughts to Ponder:

1. When you think Jesus, do you think love or religion?

2. Can I lay down my life in little ways each day for my family and close friends?

3. Is there someone in my life that consistently robs my peace or torments me that needs me to be distanced from them? This can be physically or emotionally. This is love for myself to protect my own peace.

Challenge: Lay down your life in a little way for a stranger. Let a person go in front of you at the grocery line of save half your restaurant dinner and find a homeless person and give it to them.

Write a prayer and ask the Lord to help you have desire to put feet on your faith. Lord, show me how You would specifically want me to activate my faith.

John 14

Jesus is Life

...I am the way, the truth, and the life. John 14:6

Day 67

1. Does Jesus want our hearts to be troubled.

*A troubled heart needs to be a momentary thing.

John 14:1 NKJV
"Let not your heart be troubled; you believe in God, believe also in Me.

2. He is giving us a visual picture of our future. Why is He going away?

John 14:2 NKJV
In My Father's house are many mansions; if it were not so, I would have told you. I go to prepare a place for you.

3. What is Christ doing in this verse?

John 14:3 NKJV
And if I go and prepare a place for you, I will come again and receive you to Myself; that where I am, there you may be also.

4. Where is He going?

*Isn't Jesus the way?
John 14:4 NKJV
And where I go you know, and the way you know."

5. Does Thomas understand?

John 14:5 NKJV
Thomas said to Him, "Lord, we do not know where You are going, and how can we know the way?"

6. What is the way to eternal life?

John 14:6 NKJV
Jesus said to him, "I am the way, the truth, and the life. No one comes to the Father except through Me.

7. A. If we know Christ, then who will you also know?

   B. Who is Jesus Christ?

John 14:7 NKJV
"If you had known Me, you would have known My Father also; and from now on you know Him and have seen Him."

Answers:
1. No, the Lord wants us to engage faith more than trouble.
2. Jesus is leaving this earth to go and prepare a place for us.
3. Jesus is comforting us and giving us a promise.
4. Could this be the heaven we refer to?
5. No, Thomas does not understand. So, he is questioning Jesus.
6. Jesus is the way, the truth, and the life.
7. A. Knowing Christ (salvation, peace, love...) is knowing the Father. B. Jesus Christ is God the Father incarnate (in the flesh).

Outline:
- When my heart is troubled, it is a signal to pray and activate my faith.
- There is a promise of life.
- As we rehearse the promises of God and not the troubles of this earth, we grow and mature.
- We have an eternal home with Jesus.
- I know that I have found life when I have found joy and peace. Romans 14:17

Thoughts to Ponder:
1. What temporal circumstance distracts me from feeling peaceful?

2. What people have the power to make me anxious?

3. What boundaries do I need to put in my life to protect my peace?

Challenge: Spend one day being conscious of your thoughts. Keep a running tally of how many of your thoughts line up with fear (death) and the number of thoughts that line up with peace (life). Now intentionally choose what you will and will not think. 2 Corinthians 10:4-5

Write a prayer and ask the Lord to show you what is in your life that does not line up with life and what you need to do about it if anything.

Book of John

Day 68

Believing=Greater Works

...he who believes in Me, the works that I do he will do also; and greater ...John 14:12

1. Does Phillip understand?

John 14:8 NKJV
Philip said to Him, "Lord, show us the Father, and it is sufficient for us."

2. To know Jesus is to also know who?

John 14:9 NKJV
Jesus said to him, "Have I been with you so long, and yet you have not known Me, Philip? He who has seen Me has seen the Father; so how can you say, 'Show us the Father'?

3. A. What's Jesus' question to Phillip?

   B. Who lives in Christ?

   C. Whose words does Christ speak?

   D. Whose works does Christ do?

John 14:10 NKJV
Do you not believe that I am in the Father, and the Father in Me? The words that I speak to you I do not speak on My own authority; but the Father who dwells in Me does the works.

4. A. What does Christ want the disciples to do?

B. What proves or establishes Christ deity?

*Just like our works proves or disproves that he lives in us through the Holy Spirit.
John 14:11 NKJV
Believe Me that I am in the Father and the Father in Me, or else believe Me for the sake of the works themselves.

5. A. Can we do the works Christ did?

B. What heart condition do I need to do greater works?

John 14:12 NKJV
"Most assuredly, I say to you, he who believes in Me, the works that I do he will do also; and greater works than these he will do, because I go to My Father.

6. What is the main purpose of praying in Jesus' name?

John 14:13 NKJV
And whatever you ask in My name, that I will do, that the Father may be glorified in the Son.

7. Can I ask anything if I am one with Christ?

John 14:14 NKJV
If you ask anything in My name, I will do it.

Answers:
1. No, Philip doesn't understand.
2. Knowing the heart of Jesus is knowing the Father also.
3. A. Do you believe that I am in the Father? B. The Father lives in Jesus. C. Christ speaks the words of the Father. D. Christ does the work of the Father.
4. A. Jesus wants His disciples to believe. B. Jesus's deity is established by His works.
5. A. Yes, I can do the works Jesus did and even greater works. B. I must have a believing heart.
6. So, the Father may be glorified in the Son.

7. I can ask anything.

Outline:
- The disciples are still struggling with unbelief.
- The New Testament is a new covenant and there are new things happening that don't fit with the old religious mindset.
- Jesus is expressing His oneness with His Father.
- Jesus doesn't do anything on His own. He describes how His union with the Father glorifies the Father.
- The Father enjoys being glorified in the Son. Just as He enjoys being glorified in us.
- When we walk in oneness with the Father, He shares His glory with us by answering our prayers.
- Greater works are the promises of God as we move into faith and oneness with the Father through the Holy Spirit.

Thoughts to Ponder:
1. How do I glorify the Father with my life?

2. Do I wrestle internally until I find joy, contentment, and peace?

3. Is my internal world directed by my belief in the promises of the peace of God or hyper focused on the temporal things of this world? A signal that I am temporal focused is that I am anxious or irritated and often or stuck in negative circumstances.

Challenge: Holding onto the troubles of this world makes me feel unbalanced. It is not the way the Father intended me to live. What troubles do I need to move to the altar today?

Write a prayer and ask for a heart of gratitude large enough to reshape any circumstance. Take a troubling circumstance lay it on the altar and make a grateful list of the good that has come, is coming or could come from this evil. Philippians 4:6

Book of John

Day 69

The Helper is the Holy Ghost.

...He will give you another Helper. John 14:16

1. What proves our love for Christ?

John 14:15 NKJV
"If you love Me, keep My commandments.

2. A. What will Christ pray for the Father to give us?

   B. How long will the Helper stay?

*What does abide mean? Abide – To rest or dwell to tarry or stay; to continue permanently or in the same state; to be firm and immovable.
John 14:16 NKJV
And I will pray the Father, and He will give you another Helper, that He may abide with you forever–

3. A. Is there a Spirit of Truth?

   B. Where will this spirit live after the ascension of Christ?

*We must pray to know the Holy Spirit as the Spirit of Truth and make room for it in our hearts with belief.
John 14:17 NKJV
the Spirit of truth, whom the world cannot receive, because it neither sees Him nor knows Him; but you know Him, for He dwells with you and will be in you.

4. A. Will Christ leave us comfortless?

B. Who will come to us?

John 14:18 NKJV
I will not leave you orphans; I will come to you.

5. A. Will the world recognize Christ?

B. If we believe, and we see Christ, what is the promise to us?

*I find that I must confess my unbelief as sin and ask for the help to believe. The choice is to believe or not believe. And yet, believing is so much bigger than me and I can't seem to believe without the Lord empowering me to believe.
John 14:19 NKJV
"A little while longer and the world will see Me no more, but you will see Me. Because I live, you will live also.

6. A. Who is in the Father?

B. Who are we to be in, so He can be one with us?

John 14:20 NKJV
At that day you will know that I am in My Father, and you in Me, and I in you.

7. A. If we know and study His commandments and keep them that means what?

B. What three blessings will we receive when we keep His commandments?

*It is in studying the commandments and obeying all we know to do then we will receive more understanding and belief.
John 14:21 NKJV

He who has My commandments and keeps them, it is he who loves Me. And he who loves Me will be loved by My Father, and I will love him and manifest Myself to him."

8. What is Judas (not Iscariot) asking Christ?

John 14:22 NKJV
Judas (not Iscariot) said to Him, "Lord, how is it that You will manifest Yourself to us, and not to the world?"

9. Who does Jesus say He will reveal Himself?

John 14:23 NKJV
Jesus answered and said to him, "If anyone loves Me, he will keep My word; and My Father will love him, and We will come to him and make Our home with him.

Answers:
1. Our love for Christ is proven by obedience in keeping His commandments.
2. A. Jesus prays for us to have the Helper. B. The Helper will abide in us forever.
3. A. The Holy Spirit is also the Spirit of Truth. B. The Spirit of Truth will dwell with you.
4. A. No, Jesus will not leave us comfortless. B. Jesus will come to us through the indwelling Holy Spirit.
5. A. No, the world will not recognize Christ. B. When we believe, Jesus will live in us through the Holy Spirit.
6. A. Jesus is in the Father. B. And we are to be in Jesus.
7. A. Studying His commandments means we love Jesus. B. 1. That we will be loved of our Father. 2. We will be loved by Christ. 3. He will manifest or reveal Himself to us.
8. Judas (not Iscariot) asked how can we be more likely to see you than others?
9. Jesus will reveal Himself to those who keep His words (commandments).

Outline:
- It is in tuning my heart to the Lord that I might know what to obey and be given the ability to obey.
- Obedience is not bondage. It is freedom to choose to do good. Sin is bondage that takes away our free choice.
- These verses describe the Holy Spirit as the Helper and the Spirit of Truth.
- In Christ, we are not orphans, we belong.
- When the Holy Spirit dwells in us we will feel His presence through the peace that He brings us.
- The world cannot recognize Jesus.
- The power to know Jesus is through believing.

- The power to believe is in studying the Scriptures and asking for the faith to believe.
- Keeping a pure heart to grow in our belief and keep the commandments makes room in our heart for love to dwell. As love dwells within us, Jesus will reveal more of Himself to us.
- Believing in Jesus equals revelation.
- Jesus is the Word, therefore, studying the Word reveals/manifest Jesus and draws the Spirit of Truth to us. James 4:8

Thoughts to Ponder:
1. How strongly do you desire to abide in love (Jesus)?

2. How will you know He has revealed Himself to you? Hint: It will be a felt reality in your heart.

3. Can you feel His abiding presence of the Holy Spirit?

Challenge: I challenge you to reject every thought about yourself that is not loving and kind. You cannot love others until you love yourself. Matthew 22:39; Galatians 5:14

Write a prayer and ask for the Spirit of Truth to come and abide in you.

Book of John

Day 70

Jesus is Peace

But the Helper (Comforter), the Holy Spirit, ...will teach you all things...John 14:26

1. How can you tell if a person who professes Christ doesn't love Him?

John 14:24 NKJV
He who does not love Me does not keep My words; and the word which you hear is not Mine but the Father who sent Me.

2. What was Jesus doing?

John 14:25 NKJV
"These things I have spoken to you while being present with you.

3. A. Who is the Comforter?

   B. What is the job of the Comforter/Holy Ghost?

John 14:26 NKJV
But the Helper (Comforter), the Holy Spirit, whom the Father will send in My name, He will teach you all things, and bring to your remembrance all things that I said to you.

4. A. What does Christ leave us?

   B. How do you know you have His peace?

John 14:27 NKJV

Peace, I leave with you, my peace I give to you; not as the world gives do I give to you. Let not your heart be troubled, neither let it be afraid.

5.   A. Will Jesus come again?

      B. Who is the greatest in the Trinity?

John 14:28 NKJV
You have heard Me say to you, 'I am going away and coming back to you.' If you loved Me, you would rejoice because I said, 'I am going to the Father,' for My Father is greater than I.

6.   What's the purpose of prophecy?

John 14:29 NKJV
"And now I have told you before it comes, that when it does come to pass, you may believe.

7.   Who is the prince of this world?

John 14:30 NKJV
I will no longer talk much with you, for the ruler of this world is coming, and he has nothing in Me.

8.   What does Jesus' plan to do?

*He plans to die on a cross for the sins of the world.
John 14:31 NKJV
But that the world may know that I love the Father, and as the Father gave Me commandment, so I do. Arise, let us go from here.

Answers:
    1. A person who does not love Christ doesn't keep His commandments.
    2. Jesus was speaking words to the disciples.
    3. A. The Holy Ghost is the Comforter. B. The Holy Ghost will teach us all things and bring all things to our remembrance that Christ has taught us in His Word.
    4. A. Christ will leave us peace. B. Your heart will not be troubled, nor will it be afraid.
    5. A. Yes, Jesus will come again. B. The Father is the greatest of the trinity.
    6. The purpose of prophecy is so we will believe when it comes to pass.

7. Satan is the prince of this world.
8. Jesus plans to obey the commandment of the Father.

Outline:

- If I love my sin more than I love God, I won't keep His commandments. I will pick and choose which ones to obey or believe.
- The Holy Spirit is a helper, comforter, Spirit of Truth, teacher, guide and helps me remember His words.
- I know I am a divided person when I am anxious. Oneness with Christ through the Holy Spirit brings me great peace.
- Trouble is normal. Anxiety should not be.
- Rehearsing the promises of God and not anxious thoughts is empowering.
- Jesus knew the cross was coming and was planning on trusting and obeying.

Thoughts to Ponder:

1. If I indulge complaining and grumbling am I partnering with the Holy Spirit or the Prince of this world? Philippians 2:14-15

2. Is there anyone in your life that you love enough to die for?

3. Is there anyone in your life that you love enough to live for and train in the ways of love?

Challenge: When you are troubled, settle yourself and seek peace until it comes. Do this by connecting to your breath, staying in the present moment, or rehearsing the promises of God. Then speak life over yourself and the situation.

Angie Meadows

Write a prayer and ask the Holy Spirit to teach you to calm your anxiety and rest in Him. This is how you do it.... Lord, You said Your burden is light and your yoke is easy, so this must not be mine. Matthew 11:28-30 So, if you can make something of this mess, please do because I can't.

John 15

Abiding in Christ

Abide in Me, and I in you... John 15:4

Day 71

1. A. Who is the true vine?

   B. Who is the husbandman?

*Husbandman – a farmer. A person who manages resources.
John 15:1 NKJV
"I am the true vine, and My Father is the vinedresser."

2. A. Who does the taking away?

   B. Who does the pruning?

   C. What happens if we are fruitful?

   D. Why?

* Purge – means to make free from impurities.

John 15:2 NKJV

Every branch in Me that does not bear fruit He takes away; and every branch that bears fruit He prunes, that it may bear more fruit.

3. What makes us clean?

* Clean means to have purity in our hearts.

John 15:3 NKJV

You are already clean because of the word which I have spoken to you.

4. What is the secret of bearing fruit?

* Abiding – means to be permanent and immovable in Christ to rest and dwell in him.

John 15:4 NKJV

Abide in Me, and I in you. As the branch cannot bear fruit of itself, unless it abides in the vine, neither can you, unless you abide in Me.

5. Can we bear fruit without Christ?

John 15:5 NKJV

"I am the vine; you are the branches. He who abides in Me, and I in him, bears much fruit; for without Me you can do nothing.

6. What happens to the one that does not abide in Christ?

John 15:6 NKJV

If anyone does not abide in Me, he is cast out as a branch and is withered; and they gather them and throw them into the fire, and they are burned.

7. What does it mean to ask whatever we want, and it will be done for us?

*We will know the will of God if we are abiding in Him because we will be one with Him. Christ was abiding in the Father and all His prayers were answered.
*We are to abide in Christ like Christ abided in the Father.

John 15:7 NKJV
If you abide in Me, and My words abide in you, you will ask what you desire, and it shall be done for you.

8. A. What is the purpose of bearing fruit?

   B. What makes us disciples?

John 15:8 NKJV
By this My Father is glorified, that you bear much fruit; so, you will be My disciples.

9. What is the command here?

John 15:9 NKJV
"As the Father loved Me, I also have loved you; abide in My love.

10. How do we continue in His love?

John 15:10 NKJV
If you keep My commandments, you will abide in My love, just as I have kept My Father's commandments and abide in His love.

Answers:
1. A. Jesus is the true vine. B. God, the Father, is the husbandman.
2. A. God does the taking away. B. God does the pruning. C. He purges us when we are fruitful. D. He prunes us so, we can make more fruit.
3. The Word that Jesus speaks unto us makes us clean.
4. Abiding in Christ is the secret to bearing fruit.
5. No, we cannot bear fruit without Christ.
6. A person without an identity in Christ may be cast forth like a branch and wither.
7. We may ask anything in accordance with the promises of God and according to the will of God that He reveals to us.
8. A. The purpose of bearing fruit is to glorify the Father. B. Bearing fruit and glorifying God makes us disciples.
9. The command is to continue in My love.
10. If we keep His commandments, this will empower us to continue in His love.

Outline:
- Jesus is the nourishment for believers. God is the continual overseer.
- God helps me grow through life's trials and tribulations. Nothing is wasted.

- When I bear fruit, I need to remember the cycles of life for the branch include pruning. Pruning is a good thing if I respond with patience and love.
- If I get dirty from life's struggles the Word will keep me clean.
- Abiding is Christ is a maturity skill to be learned and practiced. It requires me to quiet my heart in the Lord.
- When my heart is in tune with the Lord, I will know how to pray.
- The fruit that I bear will bring God glory.
- To continue in the love of Christ is to love myself and my neighbor and to respond to others with the patience and kindness characteristic of love.
- Obedience to all I know to do keeps my conscious clear that I may be empowered to continue growing and maturing.

Thoughts to Ponder:

1. Does abiding in Christ seem too hard? Then tell him so...

2. It is not by power or by might but by My spirit says the Lord. The continuous supply of oil is from the Word of the Lord. Zechariah 4:6 What voices need tuned out to make room for the oil to flow?

3. Do you get overwhelmed with the evil in this world and call God a liar as the prophet Jeremiah did? Jeremiah 15:18-21

Challenge: What was Jeremiah's instructions? Can you separate the evil from the good?

Write a prayer and tell the Lord what is unbearable in your life and ask Him to deliver you out of the hand of the wicked and cruel people who oppress you.

Angie Meadows

Day 72

Jesus=Joy

... that your joy may be full. John 15:11

1. What brings us the promise of joy?

John 15:11 NKJV
"These things I have spoken to you, that My joy may remain in you, and that your joy may be full.

2. What is this commandment?

John 15:12 NKJV
This is My commandment, that you love one another as I have loved you.

3. A. What did Christ do for us?

   B. What are we to do for others?

*Laying down our lives is not being a doormat but following the call of God on my life.
John 15:13 NKJV
Greater love has no one than this, than to lay down one's life for his friends.

4. What makes us Christ's friends?

John 15:14 NKJV
You are My friends if you do whatever I command you.

5. What does the Lord call us in this verse?

John 15:15 NKJV
No longer do I call you servants, for a servant does not know what his master is doing; but I have called you friends, for all things that I heard from My Father I have made known to you.

6. What are we chosen to do?

John 15:16 NKJV
You did not choose Me, but I chose you and appointed you that you should go and bear fruit, and that your fruit should remain, that whatever you ask the Father in My name He may give you.

7. What is His command?

John 15:17 NKJV
These things I command you, that you love one another.

Answers:
1. God's commandments bring the promise of joy.
2. The commandment is that you love one another as Christ loved us.
3. A. Jesus Christ laid down His life for us. B. We are to lay down our life for others.
4. If we obey His commands, we are Christ's friends.
5. We are no longer servants; we are friends.
6. We are chosen to bring forth fruit that will last and to get an answer to every prayer.
7. The command is that we love one another.

Outline:
- A promise of joy is the reward for abiding in His Word.
- Christ tunes our heart to love others.
- Laying down our lives for others is a life of service and devotion to one another.
- The friends of Jesus realize that obedience to His commands brings us freedom and goodness.
- When we go from servants to friends, we will know more of the Father's direction for our lives.
- Internal fruit is a spirit filled life of the believer in Galatians 5:22-24.
- Loving others removes our natural fleshly selfish bent.

Thoughts to Ponder:
1. The fruit of the Spirit are attitudes and characteristics that must be practiced. They do not come naturally. Choose one and practice it today: love, joy, peace, patience, kindness, goodness, faithfulness, gentleness, and self-control.

2. The spirit can be joyful that God is doing a good work in us, even when our soul is sorrowful over circumstances around us. It is a double command to rejoice. Philippians 4:4 How could I practice joy during difficulties?

Challenge: Give yourself a hug. Put your right hand on your left shoulder and your left hand on your right shoulder and say, "I am loved." Say this everyday as often as you need to do it, until your heart opens, and you feel loved.

Write a prayer and ask God to show you who needs your encouragement. Often, we get hyper focused on people who are troubled and lose sight of those in our circle that need a simple hug, affirmation, and validation.

Day 73

The world rejects Jesus.

...but I chose you out of the world...John 15:19

1. Will the world hate us?

John 15:18 NKJV
"If the world hates you, you know that it hated Me before it hated you.

2. Why does the world hate us?

John 15:19 NKJV
If you were of the world, the world would love its own. Yet because you are not of the world, but I chose you out of the world, therefore the world hates you.

3. Should we expect persecution?

John 15:20 NKJV
Remember the word that I said to you, 'A servant is not greater than his master.' If they persecuted Me, they will also persecute you. If they kept My word, they will keep yours also.

4. Do our persecutors know God?

John 15:21 NKJV
But all these things they will do to you for My name's sake, because they do not know Him who sent Me.

5. Now that Christ has come and spoken unto us, does anyone have an excuse for sin?

John 15:22 NKJV
If I had not come and spoken to them, they would have no sin, but now they have no excuse for their sin.

6. Can any religion hate Christ and say they love God?

*You can't come to God except through Jesus. John 14:6
John 15:23 NKJV
He who hates Me hates My Father also.

7. What proved Jesus' deity?

John 15:24 NKJV
If I had not done among them the works which no one else did, they would have no sin; but now they have seen and also hated both Me and My Father.

8. Does anyone have a cause to hate Christ?

John 15:25 NKJV
But this happened that the word might be fulfilled which is written in their law, 'They hated Me without a cause.'

9. A. Who is the Spirit of Truth?

   B. How will we know who has the Spirit of Truth (Comforter/Holy Ghost)?

John 15:26 NKJV
"But when the Helper comes, whom I shall send to you from the Father, the Spirit of truth who proceeds from the Father, He will testify of Me.

10. Who will bear witness of Christ?

John 15:27 NKJV
And you also will bear witness because you have been with Me from the beginning.

Answers:
1. Yes, the world will hate us.

2. The world hates us because we are chosen to do the will of God and the world is at enmity with God.
3. Yes, we should expect persecution from those who do not keep the Word of God.
4. No, persecutors do not know Father, God.
5. No, we all have the Word of God and no excuse.
6. No, Jesus and the Father are one.
7. Jesus's works was proof of His deity.
8. No, there was no cause to hate Jesus.
9. A. The Comforter, the Holy Ghost is the Spirit of Truth. B. They will testify of Jesus in their life.
10. Jesus's disciples will bear witness of Him because they have been with Him from the beginning of His ministry.

Outline:
- The world doesn't recognize Jesus because of their unbelief.
- The world will hate us for doing the will of God.
- Persecution comes from those who do not believe the Word.
- Persecutors do not know God.
- The Word will judge us, not Christ.
- Jesus proved His deity with miracles and still some refused to believe.
- There was no cause to hate Jesus, He went about doing good.
- The Holy Spirit will comfort us and help us know truth.
- We, like the disciples, will be witnesses for Jesus.

Thoughts to Ponder:
1. Are you rooted and grounded in the Word strong enough to endure when tribulation and persecution comes? Matthew 13:21

2. In Mark 10:29-30 we are promised a hundredfold of what we give up for Christ's sake. But this promise comes "with persecutions". Why do you think it comes with persecutions?

3. A godly life promises persecution. This means we will be misunderstood and even mocked. Write out 2 Timothy 3:12.

Challenge: Next time you recognize that you are mocked or persecuted for your belief in Christ, practice not personalizing it. But rejoicing that when you are weak, then He is strong. 2 Corinthians 12:10

Write a prayer and ask God to help you stand strong when you are persecuted for doing what is right and just know you are inheriting the kingdom of heaven. Matthew 5:11

John 16

Offense is stumbling!

...that you should not be made to stumble. John 16:1

Day 74

1. Why would we be offended? (John 15:18-20)

* Offended means to stumble.
John 16:1 NKJV
"These things I have spoken to you, that you should not be made to stumble.

2. Who will put us out of the synagogues and kill us?

John 16:2 NKJV
They will put you out of the synagogues; yes, the time is coming that whoever kills you will think that he offers God service.

3. Why will they do these things?

John 16:3 NKJV
And these things they will do to you because they have not known the Father nor Me.

4. Did Jesus tell them everything at the beginning?

John 16:4 NKJV
But these things I have told you, that when the time comes, you may remember that I told you of them. And these things I did not say to you at the beginning, because I was with you.

5. Where is Jesus going?

John 16:5 NKJV
"But now I go away to Him who sent Me, and none of you asks Me, 'Where are You going?'

6. How do the disciples feel?

John 16:6 NKJV
But because I have said these things to you, sorrow has filled your heart.

Answers:
1. We would naturally be offended, because the world will hate us.
2. Religious people trust in law and rules and not in Jesus Christ and don't recognize Him as Messiah and won't accept His followers.
3. Religious/legalist leaders don't have a relationship with the Father through Christ.
4. No, Jesus didn't tell them everything, because it wasn't time for them to know.
5. Jesus is going to the Father.
6. The disciples are filled with sorrow.

Outline:
- Religion trust in rules and laws.
- Religion is arrogant and political with its own agenda.
- Religion doesn't build relationships.
- Religion has a lot of hoops to jump through.
- Religion is judgmental and condemning of others and not gracious and merciful.
- I only know in part. I can't see the big picture. This is where my faith must be activated.
- When Jesus goes to the Father, He will send us the Holy Spirit so we may be one with the Son and the Father.
- Our spirit can be rejoicing in the future promises of God even as our soul is sorrowful with the troubles of this world.

Thoughts to Ponder:
1. Where should I be grieving and detaching and what should I accept. Acceptance (love) bears all things, believes all things, hopes all things, endures all things. 1 Corinthians 13:7

2. Do I identify with the rules of religion more than grace and mercy of Jesus Christ?

3. Romans 2:1,3, says as I am judging another, I am condemning myself because I do the same thing. Do I have an attitude of judging and condemning others? Listen to your grumbling... and repent. Grumbling is not patience. It's not love. It is usually judging.

Challenge: Today, recognize when you are judging others and look in the mirror and see what you are doing that is similar. God often puts people in front of me that magnify what I am doing and irritate me greatly. This is my cue to correct myself.
For example: If my children are talking back to me and I keep correcting them and it doesn't resolve, then it is probably me talking back to others that needs corrected. Can you let others have the last word?

Write a Prayer and ask the Lord to prick your spirit when you are judging another. You will hear this judgment through your complaints of another.

Day 75

Holy Spirit is Comfort

...I will send Him (Holy Spirit) to you. John 16:7

1. A. Will Christ abandon them?

   B. Who will He send them?

   C. Who is the Comforter?

John 16:7 NKJV
Nevertheless, I tell you the truth. It is to your advantage that I go away; for if I do not go away, the Helper will not come to you; but if I depart, I will send Him to you.

2. What will the Comforter do when He comes?

John 16:8 NKJV
And when He has come, He will convict the world of sin, and of righteousness, and of judgment:

3. What is their sin?

John 16:9 NKJV
of sin, because they do not believe in Me;

4. How does He convict them of righteousness?

John 16:10 NKJV
of righteousness, because I go to My Father, and you see Me no more.

5. Who is judged?

John 16:11 NKJV
of judgment, because the ruler of this world is judged.

Answers:
1. A. No, Christ will not abandon us. B. Jesus will send us the Comforter (Helper). C. The Comforter is the Holy Ghost that will live in us.
2. The Holy Ghost will reprove the world of sin, and of righteousness and judgment.
3. Jesus reproves them of sin because of their unbelief.
4. Christ is our righteousness and in Him alone can we be righteous.
5. The prince of this world is judged.

Outline:
- The Bible says the Lord will never leave me or forsake me. Hebrews 13:5
- Jesus will send me the Holy Spirit as a helper.
- The Holy Spirit empowers me to correct myself.
- The Holy Spirit empowers me to believe.
- Jesus is my righteousness.
- Without the Holy Spirit I may not be able to discern the forces of evil. Instead, I may identify with darkness or curses spoken over me.
- The Holy Spirit helps me identify with righteousness. Righteousness is simply doing what is right.

Thoughts to Ponder:
1. Do I know how to hold the presence of God? Personally, I do this by releasing all toxicity and anything that causes me suffering. I do this by moving the suffering outside of myself (usually through journaling) and identifying with the goodness of God.

2. If I am stuck in an emotion for more than two weeks, I reach out to a trusted friend or a counselor to receive help. If I rehearse bitterness and relive it, well, it grows. If I process it and release it, I grow. Are you stuck in a negative emotion?

3. Do I struggle with guilt and shame, or can I move it with my belief in the righteousness of Jesus? Isaiah 61:10 The Lord covers me in his garments of the robe of righteousness.

Challenge: Anxiety signals me that I have forgotten to believe God and that I need to activate my faith. Do I know how to activate the Holy Spirit within me to trust God in every situation?

Write a prayer and ask God to hear your prayers. Then pray, Lord, I believe; help my unbelief! Mark 9:24 It's ok to struggle with unbelief. Just confess it and keep moving forward. Believing is bigger than me. It is a work of the Holy Spirit.

Book of John

Day 76

Spirit of Truth is Understanding

...the Spirit of truth... will tell you things to come. John 16:13

1. Can we understand everything now?

John 16:12 NKJV
"I still have many things to say to you, but you cannot bear them now.

2. A. Who is the Spirit of Truth?

   B. What will the comforter do?

*Pray to learn to hear the Holy Ghost.
John 16:13 NKJV
However, when He, the Spirit of truth, has come, He will guide you into all truth; for He will not speak on His own authority, but whatever He hears He will speak; and He will tell you things to come.

3. Who shall glorify Christ?

John 16:14 NKJV
He will glorify Me, for He will take of what is Mine and declare it to you.

4. What shall the Comforter show us?

John 16:15 NKJV
All things that the Father has are mine. Therefore, I said that he will take of mine and declare it to you.

5. What future event is Jesus preparing them for?

John 16:16 NKJV
"A little while, and you will not see Me; and again a little while, and you will see Me, because I go to the Father."

6. What has Jesus been saying to them?

John 16:17 NKJV
Then some of His disciples said among themselves, "What is this that He says to us, 'A little while, and you will not see Me; and again a little while, and you will see Me'; and, 'because I go to the Father'?"

Answers:
1. No, we cannot understand everything now.
2. A. The Holy Spirit is a Comforter. B. The Holy Spirit shall speak what He hears and will show us things to come.
3. The Comforter shall glorify Jesus Christ.
4. The Comforter shall show us all things that belong to the Father and Christ.
5. Jesus is talking about His death and resurrection.
6. Jesus is telling them in a little while they will not see Him because He is going to the Father.

Outline:
- Faith supersedes understanding.
- Holy Spirit is my Comforter and teacher who will teach me what He hears and shows me things to come.
- The Holy Spirit will always glorify Jesus.
- The Holy Spirit will show us things that belong to the Father.
- Jesus is going to the Father.
- Jesus says:
1) I am not going to be here; you are going to continue my work. (John 15:5,8,14,16)
2) I am sending you the Holy Spirit to help you. (John 14:16,17,18,26; 16:7)
3) I am going away to my Father. (John 14:2,12,28;16:16,28)
4) I will return. (John 14:3; 16:16)

Thoughts to Ponder:
1. Do you feel the presence of the Holy Spirit in you?

2. Do you know how to detach from emotions and ask the Holy Spirit for wisdom in a situation?

3. Can you recognize the Holy Spirit's voice and differentiate it from your own voice?

Challenge: Ask the Lord a question and listen for the answer. If you ask a question, you will recognize when it is answered and start learning to discern His voice. The Lord will answer through Scripture, preaching, a song, another person, through an internal impression or even internal words or spontaneous thoughts. The Lord can also speak through dreams and occasionally an audible voice.

Write a prayer and ask the Lord to quiet the internal noise so you may recognize His still, small, voice.

Angie Meadows

Day 77

Answered Prayer is Joy

Ask, and you will receive, that your joy may be full. John 16:24

1. Did the disciples understand?

John 16:18 NKJV
They said therefore, "What is this that He says, 'A little while'? We do not know what He is saying."

2. Does Jesus know their questions before verbalized them?

John 16:19 NKJV
Now Jesus knew that they desired to ask Him, and He said to them, "Are you inquiring among yourselves about what I said, 'A little while, and you will not see Me; and again a little while, and you will see Me'?

3. A. Will the disciples be sad?

   B. What will happen to their sadness when they understand what is happening?

John 16:20 NKJV
Most assuredly, I say to you that you will weep and lament, but the world will rejoice; and you will be sorrowful, but your sorrow will be turned into joy.

4. What does this mean?

John 16:21 NKJV

A woman, when she is in labor, has sorrow because her hour has come; but as soon as she has given birth to the child, she no longer remembers the anguish, for joy that a human being has been born into the world.

5. A. When will sorrow be turned into joy?

   B. Can anyone take away from them this type of joy?

John 16:22 NKJV
Therefore, you now have sorrow; but I will see you again and your heart will rejoice, and your joy no one will take from you.

6. To whom will we be praying?

John 16:23 NKJV
"And in that day you will ask Me nothing. Most assuredly, I say to you, whatever you ask the Father in My name He will give you.

7. A. Does Jesus encourage us to ask for what we need?

   B. Why?

John 16:24 NKJV
Until now you have asked nothing in My name. Ask, and you will receive, that your joy may be full.

Answers:
1. No, the disciples did not understand.
2. Yes, Jesus knew their questions before they asked.
3. A. Yes, the disciples will be sad over temporal circumstances. B. Their sadness will turn to joy (cheerfulness).
4. It is a word picture of the joy the disciples will feel when they realize what is really happening.
5. A. The disciples will have joy when they see Jesus again. B. No, true joy cannot be taken away from them.
6. We will pray to God, the Father, in the name of Jesus.
7. A. Yes, we can ask for anything according to His promises. B. So, we can receive answers, and our joy may be full.

Outline:
- The disciples spent a lot of time not understanding Jesus, but they kept following.
- Jesus knew the disciples' heart.
- Temporal circumstances can make us sad. But true spiritual joy comes when we see what Jesus is doing in our lives is so much greater.
- A new mother's joy overcomes the pain of labor.
- True spiritual joy cannot be taken away.
- Let us pray to God in the name of Jesus.
- Pray and ask for what you need. It is the Lord's pleasure to answer our prayers.

Thoughts to Ponder:
1. What do I need that I haven't prayed for yet?

2. Does temporal suffering rob me of my joy?

3. Do I think my loved ones are too far gone to pray for anymore?

Challenge: Can I get a vision of what God is doing in my life that is greater than the suffering I am experiencing?

Write a prayer ask the Lord to remove anything hindering you from praying? Often, I am walking in my sorrows and need an encounter with God to experience His joy. I have already worked through forgiving others of their offenses. So, when I asked the Lord what to do with my lingering hurts, I heard the Word, "Repent". Repent, Lord, for someone else who hurt me?

The truth is that when I give away my power and agree with the hurts, I am agreeing with something inferior, and it is setting up a hiding place to contaminate other areas of my life. Now, repent and release yourself from your hurts and allow your wounds to heal and then you will be free to love again. Jesus never held an offense or an emotional wound. He released it all to the Father.

Day 78

Jesus is peace.

...but be of good cheer, I have overcome the world. John 16:33

1. A. In times past Jesus has spoken in Proverbs, how will He speak to us soon?

   B. How is He going to speak to us if He isn't here?

John 16:25 NKJV
"These things I have spoken to you in figurative language; but the time is coming when I will no longer speak to you in figurative language, but I will tell you plainly about the Father.

2. Can we go directly to the Father with our prayers?

John 16:26 NKJV
In that day you will ask in My name, and I do not say to you that I shall pray the Father for you.

3. How can we receive the ability to go straight to the Father with our prayers?

John 16:27 NKJV
for the Father Himself loves you, because you have loved Me, and have believed that I came forth from God.

4. A. Where did Jesus come from?

   B. Where is He going?

John 16:28 NKJV

I came forth from the Father and have come into the world. Again, I leave the world and go to the Father."

5. Can the disciples understand Him now?

John 16:29 NKJV
His disciples said to Him, "See, now You are speaking plainly, and using no figure of speech!

6. A. What are the disciples sure of now?

   B. Where did Jesus come from?

John 16:30 NKJV
Now we are sure that You know all things and have no need that anyone should question You. By this we believe that You came forth from God."

7. What's the question?

John 16:31 NKJV
Jesus answered them, "Do you now believe?

8. A. What is going to happen to the disciples?

   B. Will Jesus truly be left alone?

John 16:32 NKJV
Indeed, the hour is coming, yes, has now come, that you will be scattered, each to his own, and will leave Me alone. And yet I am not alone, because the Father is with Me.

9. A. What will we have in Jesus?

   B. What will we have in this world?

   C. When we have tribulation, what should our attitude be?

D. What are we to remember during tribulation?

*Joyfulness in trials and tribulations comes when a person learns to walk in the spirit and not the flesh. Then their soul can be healed from old wounds, and they can become strong in their daily walk with the Lord. With this type of maturity, their invisible God is more real than their visible world. Their heart has learned to believe, trust, and abide in Him. This is how they can genuinely be cheerful during stressful times.

John 16:33 NKJV
These things I have spoken to you, that in Me you may have peace. In the world you will have tribulation; but be of good cheer, I have overcome the world."

Answers:
1. A. Soon Jesus will speak plainly. B. Jesus speaks through the Holy Spirit in us. (John 16:13)
2. Yes, we may go directly to the Father.
3. If we love Jesus and believe He came from the Father, the Father will love us.
4. A. Jesus came from the Father. B. Jesus is going to the Father.
5. Yes, He is speaking plainly.
6. A) Christ knows all things. B) Christ came from the Father.
7. Do you now believe?
8. A. The disciples will all be scattered. B. No because the Father is with Him.
9. A. We will have peace in Jesus. B. We will have tribulation in this world. C. Our attitude can be cheerful during tribulation. D. Jesus has overcome the world, and we are in Him.

Outline:
- Jesus speaks plainly to us through the Holy Spirit.
- We have direct access to the Father through Jesus.
- If we believe in Jesus, the Father loves us.
- Christ knows all things.
- Christ came from the Father.
- Jesus isn't alone, He has the Father.
- Jesus is our peace.
- In the world there is tribulation, but with Jesus we can be overcomers.
- Ponder the thought of a *cheerful overcomer*.

Thoughts to Ponder:
1. How can I become a *cheerful overcomer* in the most devastating disappointments in my life?

2. Can I ask the Lord to take all things and turn them to my good? Romans 8:28

3. When I have peace I have the presence of God. Can I settle myself in the Word with prayer until I find peace?

Challenge: Today when an irritating challenge comes and makes you angry, practice detaching from the emotions connected to it and connecting to Christ. Christ will teach you to be a cheerful overcomer through your faith in Him.

Write a prayer and ask God for a vision for your future. The Word says that His people perish without a vision. Proverbs 29:18

John 17

It's a Finished Work.

...I have finished the work which You have given Me to do.
John 17:4

Day 79

1. A. What is Jesus doing?

   B. What is Jesus's prayer?

*This is the longest recorded prayer of Jesus.
John 17:1 NKJV
Jesus spoke these words, lifted up His eyes to heaven, and said: "Father, the hour has come. Glorify Your Son, that Your Son also may glorify You,

2. Who has the power (authority) over all flesh?

John 17:2 NKJV
as You have given Him authority over all flesh, that He should give eternal life to as many as You have given Him.

3. What is eternal life?

John 17:3 NKJV

And this is eternal life, that they may know You, the only true God, and Jesus Christ whom You have sent.

4. What is Jesus' testimony?

*We need to pray for the strength and ability to complete the work that God gives us to do.
John 17:4 NKJV
I have glorified You on the earth. I have finished the work which You have given Me to do.

5. What is Jesus asking Himself?

John 17:5 NKJV
And now, O Father, glorify Me together with Yourself, with the glory which I had with You before the world was.

*There are three states that Jesus was in:
1. Eternal pre-existence – John 1:1-2.
2. Incarnation (God the Son becoming human and yet remaining God) - John 1:14.
3. Restored glory - John 17:5.

Answers:
1. A. Jesus is praying. B. Jesus prays that God would glorify Him, and that He may glorify God.
2. Jesus has the power and authority over all flesh.
3. *Eternal life* is that we know the one and only true God and Jesus whom He sent.
4. Jesus testifies that He has completed the work He was given to do.
5. Jesus is asking for a state of restored glory.

Outline:
- Jesus shows us the need for prayer.
- Prayer ushers in the glory of God through faith.
- Faith prays.
- Jesus gives eternal life.
- Eternal life is that I may know the one true God through Jesus His Son.

Thoughts to Ponder:
1. It was great gain for Jesus to humble Himself unto death. Philippians 2:8 Can you humble yourself, surrender and trust God with all things.?

2. Are you confident that God who has begun a good work in you will finish it? Philippians 1:6

3. Do I know when to strive and when to rest?

Challenge: What would it look like to make myself of no reputation and become the Lord's servant and let Him be my Master? Philippians 2:7

Write a prayer and ask God to give you a vision and help you finish the work and fulfill all that is written in the book of you. Lord, let me leave nothing undone. Hebrews 10:7

Book of John

Day 80

Receiving, Keeping & Believing

...they have kept Your word...and they have received them... they have believed. John 17:6,8.

1. A. Who is Jesus praying for now?

   B. What is a condition for being a disciple?

John 17:6 NKJV
"I have manifested Your name to the men whom You have given Me out of the world. They were Yours, You gave them to Me, and they have kept Your word.

2. What things do the disciples know about the things God, the Father, gave to Jesus?

John 17:7 NKJV
Now they have known that all things which You have given Me are from You.

3. What did the disciples believe?

John 17:8 NKJV
For I have given to them the words which You have given Me; and they have received them, and have known surely that I came forth from You; and they have believed that You sent Me.

4. A. Does Jesus pray for the world?

   B. Who does Jesus pray for in this verse?

John 17:9 NKJV

"I pray for them. I do not pray for the world but for those whom You have given Me, for they are Yours.

5. Who is Christ glorified in?

John 17:10 NKJV
And all Mine are Yours, and Yours are Mine, and I am glorified in them.

Answers:
1. A. Jesus is praying for His disciples. B. The disciples keep His Word.
2. The disciples know that all things Jesus has been given are from God.
3. The disciples believed that Jesus came from God.
4. A. No, Jesus excludes the world from His prayers. B. Jesus prays for the ones God has given Him.
5. Christ is glorified in all those that belong to Him.

Outline:
- Jesus prays for us.
- We are His disciples as we keep His Word.
- The disciple's believed Jesus was the Messiah from God.
- Jesus makes a difference between the world and His disciples.
- Those who belong to Jesus will glorify His name.

Thoughts to Ponder:
1. When I am disappointed and feel like the Lord has betrayed me, can I renounce that lie and stand still and just glorify Him?

2. Do I believe that all things can work together for good for those that are called according to His purpose? Romans 8:28

3. Can I humble myself when I have sinned and ask God to redeem the situation and restore me to Him to glorify His name…. no matter what?

Challenge: Humility is letting God do a work in me that I am unable to do for myself. Today, release any habitual sin or addiction to the Lord and ask Him to empower you to recover yourself. I cannot do this from a position of shame and guilt.

That is false humility. I am to do this by repenting and returning and then being confident in Him and resting. Isaiah 30:15

Write a prayer and ask the Lord to help you receive His Word and keep it.

Day 81

We are one.

...Holy Father, keep through Your name those whom You have given Me, that they may be one as We are. John 17:11

1. A. Who does He want to be one with Him?

   B. Jesus and whom are one?

John 17:11 NKJV
Now I am no longer in the world, but these are in the world, and I come to You. Holy Father, keep through Your name those whom You have given Me, that they may be one as We are.

2. Why was Judas called the "son of perdition"?

*Judas regretted his actions and repented unto remorse, shame, guilt, self-condemnation and finally self-destruction.
John 17:12 NKJV
While I was with them in the world, I kept them in Your name. Those whom You gave Me I have kept; and none of them is lost except the son of perdition, that the Scripture might be fulfilled.*

3. For what purpose is Jesus speaking these things?

*It's His joy we need.
John 17:13 NKJV
But now I come to You, and these things I speak in the world, that they may have My joy fulfilled in themselves.*

4. A. Why would we be hated?

B. Are we of this world?

C. Why was Jesus hated?

John 17:14 NKJV
I have given them Your word; and the world has hated them because they are not of the world, just as I am not of the world.

Answers:
1. A. Jesus wants believers to be one with Him. B. Jesus and the Father are one.
2. Judas was a divided man with his own agenda. He dwelled in self-condemnation, guilt, and shame and not in surrender and humility in Christ.
3. Jesus speaks these things that they may have His joy fulfilled in themselves.
4. A. We are hated because we have the Word. B. No, we are not of this world. C. Many hated Jesus because He was not of this world.

Outline:
- Judas greed-thief-betrayal-suicide.
- A divided man is ripe for Satan to manipulate.
- When I refuse grace, I am stuck in my sin.
- We have the Word living in us.
- We don't belong to this world.
- We belong to Jesus.

Thoughts to Ponder:
1. Guilt, shame and self-condemnation is remaining under the law. When we are under grace, *it is finished*. We don't need to martyr ourselves to pay for our sin. Judas was a picture of the law that condemns. Peter was a picture of grace that restores. Do you identify with Judas or Peter? Do you live in condemnation or grace?

2. Is there any toxic emotion you are stuck in? Maybe you have been stuck in grieving or sadness so long that you identify with the emotion and not with the promises of God. Today, what would it look like to identify with hope?

3. Was there an event or situation in your life that feels like a heavy burden? What does Jesus say to do about it? Matthew 11:28-30

Challenge: Grace and peace flow together. If you want more peace, receive more grace from God. *Grace unto you and peace from God our Father and the Lord Jesus Christ. 2 Thessalonians 1:2* Sit quietly and tune your heart to be kind and gracious to yourself that you may be a vessel to hold the peace of God.

Write a total surrender prayer of faith like the Old Testament Job. Lord, though you slay me, yet will I hope in you. Job 13:15

Book of John

Day 82

His Word is Truth

Sanctify them by Your truth. Your word is truth. John 17:17

1. How does Jesus pray for us?

John 17:15 NKJV
I do not pray that You should take them out of the world, but that You should keep them from the evil one.

2. Are believers of this world?

John 17:16 NKJV
They are not of the world, just as I am not of the world.

3. How are we sanctified?

*<u>Sanctified</u> – means we are separated to consecrate ourselves to God wholly for his use.
John 17:17 NKJV
Sanctify them by Your truth. Your word is truth.

4. Where are we being sent?

John 17:18 NKJV
As You sent Me into the world, I also have sent them into the world.

5. A. What is Jesus doing as an example for us?

B. What does he want us to do?

John 17:19 NKJV
And for their sakes I sanctify Myself, that they also may be sanctified by the truth.

6. For whom is Jesus praying?

John 17:20 NKJV
"I do not pray for these alone, but also for those who will believe in Me through their word;

Answers:
1. Jesus does not pray that we would be taken out of this world, but that we would be kept from evil.
2. No, believers are not of this world.
3. We are sanctified through *truth of the word*.
4. Jesus is sending me into this world.
5. A. Jesus is setting Himself apart for God's use and sanctifying Himself. B. Jesus wants us to follow His example and sanctify ourselves.
6. Jesus is praying for all future believers.

Outline:
- We are in this world but can be kept from evil.
- *Studying the Word is our superpower.*
- Sanctification is a process of being set apart.
- Preceding sanctification is a washing of regeneration of the soul (flesh) and a renewing of the Holy Ghost. Titus 3:5
- Jesus prays for us.

Thoughts to Ponder:
1. Is it comforting to know that Jesus is praying for you?

2. Counting trials and tribulations <u>all joy</u> is a <u>spiritual maturity skill</u>. This comes from rehearsing, ruminating, and meditating on the Word of God and not on our temporal problems. James 1:2 Now recall a troubling circumstance and practice feeling joy.

3. What is the promise when I meditate on God's Word? Psalm 1:2-3

Challenge:
Once emotions are processed and removed from a situation, we cannot be manipulated by them but can grow in wisdom. Move any toxic emotion to the altar and ask God to heal your doublemindedness and give you wisdom. James 1:5-8

Write a prayer and ask God to give you unwavering faith in the face of any difficulty.

Day 83

One with Christ is One with Love

...as You, Father, are in Me, and I in You; that they also may be one in Us. John 17:21

1. With whom does Christ want us to be one?

John 17:21 NKJV
that they all may be one, as You, Father, are in Me, and I in You; that they also may be one in Us, that the world may believe that You sent Me.

2. What does Jesus give us when we are one?

John 17:22 NKJV
And the glory which You gave Me I have given them, that they may be one just as We are one:

3. What is the purpose of us becoming one?

John 17:23 NKJV
I in them, and You in Me; that they may be made perfect in one, and that the world may know that You have sent Me, and have loved them as You have loved Me.

4. Can you find the statement that says Jesus was before creation?

John 17:24 NKJV
"Father, I desire that they also whom You gave Me may be with Me where I am, that they may behold My glory which You have given Me; for You loved Me before the foundation of the world.

5. A. Does the world know or recognize the righteous Father?

John 17:25 NKJV
O righteous Father! The world has not known You, but I have known You; and these have known that You sent Me.

6. What is Jesus praying to be in us?

John 17:26 NKJV
And I have declared to them Your name, and will declare it, that the love with which You loved Me may be in them, and I in them."

Answers:
1. Jesus Christ wants us to be one with other believers and one with Him and the Father.
2. Jesus gives us the glory that the Father gave Him.
3. So, the world may know that God has sent Christ, and that God loves us.
4. Jesus pre-existed in the world. "You loved Me from before the foundation of the world."
5. No, the world does not recognize Him.
6. Jesus is asking for the love to be in us as He is in us.

Outline:
- Jesus prays for us to be one with them.
- The Lord shares His glory with us.
- God sent His Son.
- God loves us.
- Jesus existed before the world was created.
- The world will not recognize Jesus.
- God is love and He wants us full of healthy love.

Thoughts to Ponder:
1. If <u>God is love</u>, then when we have a heart full of love who is in unity with us? 1 John 4:8,16

2. Becoming one with the Father through Jesus requires the infilling of the Holy Spirit. It is vitally important that we are not careless but ask God to remove all hinderances to our oneness with Him.

3. Indulging anger, irritation, frustration, or impatience will divide my heart and quench the Holy Spirit. 1 Thessalonians 5:19 What are you allowing in your life that would quench the Holy Spirit?

Challenge: Healthy love is described in 1 Corinthians 13:1-7 If I am usurping others' lessons and moving their mountains, this is most likely because I don't want to watch them to suffer. Healthy love makes sure a baby chick does the work to make their wings strong. If I remove their shell, the baby chick will die. Who do you need to take a step back from and let them strengthen themselves through life's struggles?

Write a prayer and ask God for the *grace* to love others enough to let them suffer from the consequences of their own poor choices.
*Verbally affirm and encourage others. A good rule is to not do anything for an immature person that won't work a job or is squandering their resources. Others will not mature if I do it for them. They should be supporting themselves and managing their own money.

John 18

Betrayal of Jesus by Judas.

"I am He." John 18:5

Day 84

1. A. Who was Jesus with?

   B. Where did they go?

John 18:1 NKJV
When Jesus had spoken these words, He went out with His disciples over the Brook Kidron, where there was a garden, which He and His disciples entered.

2. A. Did Jesus go there often?

   B. Did Judas know where Jesus would be?

John 18:2 NKJV
And Judas, who betrayed Him, also knew the place; for Jesus often met there with His disciples.

3. A. Who did Judas take with him to the garden to find Jesus?

B. What did they bring with them?

John 18:3 NKJV
Then Judas, having received a detachment of troops, and officers from the chief priests and Pharisees, came there with lanterns, torches, and weapons.

4. Did Jesus know all things?

John 18:4 NKJV
Jesus therefore, knowing all things that would come upon Him, went forward and said to them, "Whom are you seeking?"

5. A. Whom were they seeking?

B. What did Jesus' answer?

John 18:5 NKJV
They answered Him, "Jesus of Nazareth." Jesus said to them, "I am He." And Judas, who betrayed Him, also stood with them.

6. What happened to the men when Jesus answered?

John 18:6 NKJV
Now when He said to them, "I am He," they drew back and fell to the ground.

7. A. Jesus asked what again?

B. What did they say?

John 18:7 NKJV
Then He asked them again, "Whom are you seeking?" And they said, "Jesus of Nazareth."

Answers:
1. A. Jesus was with His disciples. B. Jesus and His disciples went over the brook of Kidron to a garden.

2. A. Yes, Jesus went there often. B. Yes, Judas knew where He would be.
3. A. Judas took a band of men, (soldiers) and officers from the chief priests and Pharisees. B. They brought lanterns, torches, and weapons.
4. Yes, Jesus knew all things.
5. A. They were seeking Jesus of Nazareth. B. Jesus answered, "I Am He."
6. They went backward and fell to the ground.
7. A. Whom do you seek? B. They said, Jesus of Nazareth.

Outline:
- Jesus is with His disciples at a garden over the brook Kidron.
- Judas knew where Jesus would be.
- Judas brought religious leaders and soldiers with Him to identify Jesus for capture.
- Jesus knew why Judas had come. He knew the motives of the religious leaders and soldiers that had come with Judas and yet He asked a question. Do you suppose He wanted them to validate their actions with their words?
- Those who come to arrest Jesus all fell to the ground when Jesus spoke, "I Am He."
- Again, He asked a question for them to validate their intentions with their words.

Thoughts to Ponder:
1. Pride blocks belief. Humility and faith are intricately intertwined. Matthew 8:5-10

2. Humbling myself is casting my cares on Him because He cares for me. It is wearing His garment of humility. Write out the instructions from 1 Peter 5:5-7

3. Write out more instructions from 1 Peter 5:8-9.

Challenge: Rehearse the *promise* in 1 Peter 5:10

Write a prayer and ask the Lord to help you to humble yourself and repent when you are contentious with others. Then to give you the wisdom to know which advice to follow. *Where there is strife, there is pride, but wisdom is found in those who take advice. Proverbs 13:10*

Book of John

Day 85

Jesus protects his own.

"I have told you that I am He. ...let these go their way,"
John 18:8

1. Who was Jesus telling them to let go?

John 18:8 NKJV
Jesus answered, "I have told you that I am He. Therefore, if you seek Me, let these go their way,"

2. Why did Jesus say to let the disciples go?

John 18:9 NKJV
that the saying might be fulfilled which He spoke, "Of those whom You gave Me I have lost none."

3. What did Simon Peter do?

John 18:10 NKJV
Then Simon Peter, having a sword, drew it and struck the high priest's servant, and cut off his right ear. The servant's name was Malchus.

4. A. What was Jesus's response to Peter?

B. Do you think Peter understand what cup the Father had given Jesus to drink?

John 18:11 NKJV
So, Jesus said to Peter, "Put your sword into the sheath. Shall I not drink the cup which My Father has given Me?"

5. What did the men do to Jesus?

John 18:12 NKJV
Then the detachment of troops and the captain and the officers of the Jews arrested Jesus and bound Him.

6. Who did they take Jesus to see?

John 18:13 NKJV
And they led Him away to Annas first, for he was the Father-in-law of Caiaphas who was high priest that year.

Answers:
1. Jesus was telling them to let His disciples go.
2. Jesus said this so the saying may be fulfilled that Jesus did not lose any of them that God gave Him.
3. Simon Peter drew a sword and cut off the ear of the high priest's servant.
4. A. When Peter cut off the ear of the high priest's servant Jesus said put your sword into the sheath. B. No, Peter did not want Jesus to go to the cross.
5. The men bound Jesus.
6. They took Jesus to see Annas, the Father-in-law of Caiaphas, the high priest.

Outline:
- Jesus won't lose any of us that belong to Him.
- Consistently throughout the book of John prophecy is fulfilled.
- Peter is consistently getting ahead of Jesus and is impulsive.
- Peter did not want His master to go to the cross. Matthew 16:14-25
- Peter thought if he had a sword that he should use it.
- For the disciples to watch their teacher be bound and taken away must have made them feel powerless.
- The disciples did not understand until later when they remembered all that He had said to them.

Thoughts to Ponder:
1. Betrayal is a hard thing. Here is a space to identify with Jesus on the ways you have been betrayed. The Holy Spirit has highlighted 5 levels of betrayal.

    A. Gossip/Slander/False Accusations.
    B. Denial of Affection/Avoidance.
    C. Un-justly Criticizes.
    D. Abandons/Neglects.
    E. Betrayal with lies and manipulation.

    Betrayal is a part of life. We all experience betrayal. Now what will you do about it and how many people do you let back in your life to continue to betray you?

What level of loyalty do you require for those you allow near your heart?

2. Some can betray us unintentionally. They can get caught up with others who triangulate them to betray us.
- Identify long term friends who are safe to confront, who have unintentionally hurt you and forgive them.
- Identify your Peter's that are impulsive, immature and may have denied you and left you in your time of need because of their fear.

3. Others, betray because of darkened heart motives. Maybe they are intimidated by us. Maybe, they are jealous. Maybe, it has nothing to do with us, but they do this to anyone they target in their path. These cannot be trusted and must not be given the power to repeatedly wound us. We must not believe their lies or internalize their condemnation.
- Identify your Judas that doesn't need access to your heart again. This person may be in your life, but don't give them power to hurt you. *You can love them with your head and not your heart and give them strong boundaries.* This is healthy.

Challenge: Recognize any heart attitudes (betrayal-bitterness) you have towards others which may fall in one of the five categories of betrayal and repent and ask God for the strength to change. Habitual betrayal of others is a personality defect and cannot be changed without deep repentance. Impulsivity is just immature and needs an accountability partner.

Angie Meadows

Write a prayer and ask the Lord to give you strength when you must drink life's bitter cup and to trust Him more and more ...no matter what you are going through.

Book of John

Day 86

Peter lies.

"You are not also one of this Man's disciples, are you?" He said, "I am not." John 18:17

1. Who had prophesied that it was expedient that one man should die for the people?

John 18:14 NKJV
Now it was Caiaphas who advised the Jews that it was expedient that one man should die for the people.

2. Who followed Jesus?

John 18:15 NKJV
And Simon Peter followed Jesus, and so did another disciple. Now that disciple was known to the high priest and went with Jesus into the courtyard of the high priest.

3. Who went and got Peter who was standing by the outside door?

John 18:16 NKJV
But Peter stood at the door outside. Then the other disciple, who was known to the high priest, went out and spoke to her who kept the door, and brought Peter in.

4. A. Who was the keeper of the door?

B. What did she ask Peter?

C. What did Peter answer?

John 18:17 NKJV
Then the servant girl who kept the door said to Peter, "You are not also one of this Man's disciples, are you?" He said, "I am not."

5. A. Where was Peter standing?

   B. Who was Peter with?

John 18:18 NKJV
Now the servants and officers who had made a fire of coals stood there, for it was cold, and they warmed themselves. And Peter stood with them and warmed himself.

Answers:
1. Caiaphas, the high priest, gave a prophecy about the death of the Messiah.
2. Simon Peter and another disciple (probably John) followed Jesus.
3. The other disciple, (maybe John), who knew the door keeper.
4. A. A damsel or servant girl was the keeper of the door.
B. The servant girl asked Peter are you not one of Jesus's disciples? C. Peter lied and said, "I am not."
5. A. Peter was standing by a fire of coals. B. Peter was standing with servants and officers (unbelievers).

Outline:
- The high priest had an anointing to prophecy over things he probably didn't understand. Our pastors may have the very same anointing, even as fallible men.
- A couple of the disciples followed Jesus but did not have the strength of the Holy Spirit living in them yet.
- All the disciples were probably sad, confused, and afraid.
- Peter was afraid of a servant girl. He was fearful enough of the circumstances to lie.

Thoughts to Ponder:
1. If you are in domestic violence, an emotionally abusive relationship or suffered as a child this way, you probably spontaneously lie to protect yourself. In what circumstances do you feel you need to lie for protection?

2. Do we always need to tell the truth?

What if the truth will be weaponized and used against us? What should we do then?

3. Rahab, the harlot, lied to protect the Israelites spies from the greater sin of murder and God called her righteous. Joshua 2:2-7; Hebrews 11:31; James 2:25. The Bible declares Rahab had faith and she was justified by her works. Do you consider this acceptable?

What about when the Germans lied to hide the Jews in the Holocaust? Was that right or wrong?

Challenge: What would it look like to stand strong during persecution?

Write a prayer and ask the Lord for the discernment to know when to speak boldly, when to be silent, when to hide yourself, and what to do when you stand before wicked unbelievers.

Day 87

Fear of man denies Christ.

Peter then denied again...John 18:27

1. What questions did the high priest ask Jesus?

John 18:19 NKJV
The high priest then asked Jesus about His disciples and His doctrine.

2. A. What was Jesus's answer?

   B. Did Jesus teach anything in secret?

John 18:20 NKJV
Jesus answered him, "I spoke openly to the world. I always taught in synagogues and in the temple, where the Jews always meet, and in secret I have said nothing.

3. Jesus tells the high priest to do what?

John 18:21 NKJV
Why do you ask Me? Ask those who have heard Me what I said to them. Indeed, they know what I said."

4. A. How did one of the officers perceive Jesus's answer?

   B. What did he do to Jesus?

John 18:22 NKJV

And when He had said these things, one of the officers who stood by struck Jesus with the palm of his hand, saying, "Do You answer the high priest like that?"

5. A. Did Jesus think He had spoken evil?

   B. So what does Jesus ask the officer?

John 18:23 NKJV
Jesus answered him, "If I have spoken evil, bear witness of the evil; but if well, why do you strike Me?"

6. How was Jesus treated?

John 18:24 NKJV
Then Annas sent Him bound to Caiaphas the high priest.

7. A. As Peter was warming himself what was he asked?

   B. How did Peter answer?

John 18:25 NKJV
Now Simon Peter stood and warmed himself. Therefore, they said to him, "You are not also one of His disciples, are you?" He denied it and said, "I am not!"

8. Who else recognized Peter?

John 18:26 NKJV
One of the servants of the high priest, a relative of him whose ear Peter cut off, said, "Did I not see you in the garden with Him?"

9. A. What did Peter say?

   B. Then what happened?

John 18:27 NKJV

Peter then denied again; and immediately a rooster crowed.

Answers:
1. The high priest asked about His disciples and about His doctrine.
2. A. I always spoke openly and always taught in the synagogue. B. No, Jesus did not hide His teachings.
3. Jesus tells the high priest to ask the people what they had heard Him teach.
4. A. The officer perceived Jesus' answer as disrespectful. B. The officer slapped Jesus with an open hand.
5. A. No, Jesus does not think He spoke evil. B. Jesus asked the officer, why have you hit Me?
6. Jesus was bound like a criminal.
7. A. Peter was asked, are you one of His disciples? B. Peter responded and said, I am not.
8. One of the servants of the high priest recognized Peter.
9. A. Peter denied knowing Jesus again. B. Then the cock (rooster) crowed.

Outline:
- Jesus was being questioned by the high priest and was very evasive with His answers and didn't defend Himself.
- Jesus seemed disrespectful with His answers but was really fulfilling prophecy. Isaiah 53:7; Act 8:32
- The officer slapped Jesus and felt justified in doing so.
- Jesus had already told Peter that He was not only not loyal enough to die for Him but that He would deny Him three times before the rooster crowed.

Thoughts to Ponder:
1. Is there things in God's Word that makes us want to lash out like the officer did with Jesus?

2. Jesus had told Peter that he would deny him three times before the rooster crowed and Peter did not believe it. What are you struggling with in your heart that would be a denial of your Christianity?

3. Is there anything you believe that you would die for?

Challenge: How could you prepare to deal with the fear of persecution for your faith in Jesus?

Write a prayer and ask the Lord to purify your heart and fill it with His Holy Spirit that your belief may be stronger than your fears.

Angie Meadows

Day 88

Name Calling is Abuse.

"If He were not an <u>evildoer</u>, we would not have delivered Him up to you." John 18:30

1. A. Where did they take Jesus next?

   B. Would the Jewish leaders go into the hall?

   C. Why not?

   D. Did they recognize that the murder they were planning would defile them?

   E. If they were defiled, what could they not do?

John 18:28 NKJV
Then they led Jesus from Caiaphas to the Praetorium, and it was early morning. But they themselves did not go into the Praetorium, lest they should be defiled, but that they might eat the Passover.

2. A. Who was judging Jesus in the hall of judgment?

   B. What does Pilate ask?

John 18:29 NKJV
Pilate then went out to them and said, "What accusation do you bring against this Man?"

3. What did they call Jesus?

* This was an abuse tactic of name calling.
John 18:30 NKJV
They answered and said to him, "If He were not an evildoer, we would not have delivered Him up to you."

4. A. What was Pilate's answer to the Jews?

   B. Why could they not do this?

John 18:31 NKJV
Then Pilate said to them, "You take Him and judge Him according to your law." Therefore, the Jews said to him, "It is not lawful for us to put anyone to death,"

5. Had Jesus predicted how He would die?

John 18:32 NKJV
that the saying of Jesus might be fulfilled which He spoke, signifying by what death He would die.

6. What did Pilate ask Jesus?

John 18:33 NKJV
Then Pilate entered the Praetorium again, called Jesus, and said to Him, "Are You the King of the Jews?"

Answers:

1. A. They took Jesus to the hall of judgment. B. No, they would not go into the hall. C. They thought they would be defiled. D. No, they thought they were justified in crucifying Jesus according to their laws, He had blasphemed. E. They could not eat the Passover if they defiled themselves in a certain way to break their laws.
2. A. Pilate, a Roman Leader, was judging Jesus in the hall of judgment. B. Pilate asked what was the accusations against this man?
3. They called Jesus a malefactor or an evildoer.

4. A. Pilate answered and said judge Him by your own law. B. They could not put Jesus to death because their law did not allow them to condemn a man to death without Pilate's permission.

5. Yes, it was prophesied in the Old Testament and Jesus had told His disciples how He would die and be resurrected.

6. Pilate asked Jesus if He was the King of the Jews?

Outline:
- The crime Jesus was accused of was making Himself equal with God.
- Jesus would not defend Himself.
- It was Jesus's time to die. He was the pure and spotless Passover Lamb.
- Pilate couldn't find fault with Jesus and was trying to get them to judge Jesus.
- They didn't want to judge Him, they had already done that, the Jewish religious leaders wanted permission to crucify Him.
- Jesus was surely the King of the Jews.

Thoughts to Ponder:
1. Do you feel accepted by other believers?

2. Have you known the church to be a safe space for you and your family? Do you have a safe place inside of yourself?

3. Are there places you feel the Holy Spirit has led you that didn't turn out the way you expected?

Challenge: The crucifixion is certainly a strange way to honor the only begotten Son of God. The Lord has a way of prying my fingers off the things I love and gives me the opportunity to trust Him more each day. This is a very hard thing, until I do it. Then, it releases me from stress and fear and brings me a heart of peace. What do you need to release to the Lord today?

Book of John

Write a prayer and ask the Lord to show you how to hide beneath the shelter of his wings. Psalm 91:1

Angie Meadows

Day 89

Jesus, King of the Jews

Jesus answered, "My kingdom is not of this world." John 18:36

1. Jesus asked Pilate what?

John 18:34 NKJV
Jesus answered him, "Are you speaking for yourself about this, or did others tell you this concerning Me?"

2. A. Was Pilate a Jew?

   B. Who wanted him killed?

John 18:35 NKJV
Pilate answered, "Am I a Jew? Your own nation and the chief priests have delivered You to me. What have You done?"

3. A. Is Jesus's kingdom of this world?

   B. If it were what would his followers do?

John 18:36 NKJV
Jesus answered, "My kingdom is not of this world. If My kingdom were of this world, my servants would fight, so that I should not be delivered to the Jews; but now My kingdom is not from here."

4. A. What is Pilate trying to understand?

B. Why was Jesus born?

C. Who can hear and understand Jesus's words?

John 18:37 NKJV
Pilate therefore said to Him, "Are You a king then?" Jesus answered, "You say rightly that I am a king. For this cause I was born, and for this cause I have come into the world, that I should bear witness to the truth. Everyone who is of the truth hears My voice."

5. A. What was Pilate's question?

B. What was Pilate's judgment of Jesus?

John 18:38 NKJV
Pilate said to Him, "What is truth?" And when he had said this, he went out again to the Jews, and said to them, "I find no fault in Him at all.

6. What was Pilate trying to do?

John 18:39 NKJV
"But you have a custom that I should release someone to you at the Passover. Do you therefore want me to release to you the King of the Jews?"

7. A. Who did the people choose to be released at the Passover?

B. Who was Barabbas?

John 18:40 NKJV
Then they all cried again, saying, "Not this Man, but Barabbas!" Now Barabbas was a robber. John 19:1 NKJV
So then Pilate took Jesus and scourged Him.

Answers:
1. Jesus asked Pilate is this your own idea or is this what others have told you?
2. A. No, Pilate is a Roman leader. B. The Jews wanted Jesus killed.
3. A. No, his kingdom is not of this world. B. His followers would fight that he should not be delivered unto the Jews.

4. A. Pilate is trying to understand if Jesus is a king? B. Jesus was born to die for our sins. C. Everyone that is of the truth can hear and understand Jesus's words.
5. A. Pilate asked what is truth? B. Pilate said, I find no fault in him.
6. Pilate was trying to release Jesus.
7. A. The people wanted Barabbas released. B. Barabbas was a robber.

Outline:
- Even the Roman leader, Pilate, knows that Jesus is the King of the Jews.
- The Jews wanted Jesus killed but could not do it without the Roman Government's approval.
- Jesus's kingdom is not of this world.
- When others cannot hear or understand the words I speak about Jesus, they are not of the truth.
- The religious leaders blocked the truth with their pride, and they trusted in their laws.
- Pilate found nothing in Jesus worthy of death.
- Pilate was trying to release Jesus.
- Barabbas was a common thief and the Jews thought he was more valuable than their Messiah.
- Truth was certainly hidden from them.
- Jesus was born to be the perfect sacrificial lamb and to die for our sins.

Thoughts to Ponder:
1. Do you understand that your sins are forgiven to be remembered no more? Isaiah 43:25

2. Do you know your sins are as far as the east is from the west? Psalm 103:12

3. If Satan is the accuser and I am accusing myself with my own harsh internal critic, then am I aligning myself with God or Satan? Revelations 12:10

Challenge: For one day do not think a negative critical thought about yourself or anyone else.

Write a prayer and ask the Lord to heal your close family and friends. Pray for them by name.

John 19

Jesus the Sinless Lamb of God.

Pilate ... said to them, ... I find no fault in Him. John 19:4

Day 90

1. What did Pilate do to Jesus?

*This fulfilled prophecy Isaiah 53:5
He was whipped in the Roman style which was more severe than the Jewish way. Scourging or whipping often preceded crucifixion. The Roman flagellum consisted of a whip, split into several strips, into which sharp bones were embedded to cut the flesh.
John 19:1 NKJV
So then Pilate took Jesus and scourged Him.

2. Why would the soldiers put on Jesus?

John 19:2 NKJV
And the soldiers twisted a crown of thorns and put it on His head, and they put on Him a purple robe.

3. Who were the soldiers hitting with their hands?

John 19:3 NKJV
Then they said, "Hail, King of the Jews!" And they struck Him with their hands.

4. A. What was Pilate's motive in his words?

B. Did Pilate find any fault in Jesus?

John 19:4 NKJV
Pilate then went out again, and said to them, "Behold, I am bringing Him out to you, that you may know that I find no fault in Him."

5. Why did they put the crown of thorns and the purple robe on Jesus?

*Tactic used for humiliation and abuse was mockery.
John 19:5 NKJV
Then Jesus came out, wearing the crown of thorns and the purple robe. And Pilate said to them, "Behold the Man!"

Answers:
1. Pilate had Jesus whipped.
2. The soldiers were mocking Him because He was called King of the Jews and twisted a thorns vine for a crown and put a purple robe or open wounds.
3. The soldiers were hitting Jesus with their hands.
4. A. Pilate was hoping they would see Jesus beaten and be satisfied to let Him go.
B. No, Pilate found no fault in Jesus.
5. The crown of thorns and purple robe was to mock Jesus.

Outline:
- Pilate hoped the scourging would bring pity for Jesus and the crowd would be satisfied, but they were not.
- The soldiers mocked Jesus. They mentally and emotionally tortured him.
- The soldiers made fun of striking Jesus.
- Pilate could find no fault in Jesus.
- The persecutors had no mercy for their victim.
- The people did not seem to care if Jesus was guilty or innocent.

Thoughts to Ponder:
1. If there is a group at work gossiping or slandering the boss, will you join in or refuse to participate?

2. How much boss bashing from others will you tolerate before you speak up or remove yourself?

3. Can your employer count on you to come to them with a problem and a potential solution?

Challenge: Today refuse to participate in gossip or slander. What words would you need to be prepared to say to stop friends, family, or co-workers, from these behaviors? The rule is if I am not part of the problem or part of the solution, then I am to remove myself from the conversation.

Write a prayer and ask the Lord to show you if you have been a part in hurting anyone with false accusations. If so, ask the Lord to show you if there is any restitution you could do. A simple act of kindness could undo the injustice.

Book of John

Day 91

The Lamb is Silent before His Oppressors.

But Jesus gave him no answer... John 19:9

1. A. Who was the main people leading the cry to crucify Jesus?

    B. Again, what did Pilate say?

John 19:6 NKJV
Therefore, when the chief priests and officers saw Him, they cried out, saying, "Crucify Him, crucify Him!" Pilate said to them, "You take Him and crucify Him, for I find no fault in Him."

2. Why did they want to kill Jesus?

John 19:7 NKJV
The Jews answered him, "We have a law, and according to our law He ought to die, because He made Himself the Son of God."

3. What's going on in Pilate's head now?

John 19:8 NKJV
Therefore, when Pilate heard that saying, he was the more afraid,

4. A. What's Pilate doing now?

    B. What does Jesus do?

*This fulfills Isaiah 53:7 prophecy.
John 19:9 NKJV
and went again into the Praetorium, and said to Jesus, "Where are You from?" But Jesus gave him no answer.

5. What is Pilate doing now?

John 19:10 NKJV
Then Pilate said to Him, "Are You not speaking to me? Do You not know that I have power to crucify You, and power to release You?"

6. Who gave Pilate power?

    Who had the greater sin?

John 19:11 NKJV
Jesus answered, "You could have no power at all against Me unless it had been given you from above. Therefore, the one who delivered Me to you has the greater sin."

Answers:
1. A. The chief priests and officers were the main people leading the cry to crucify Jesus. B. Again, Pilate says he finds no fault in Jesus.
2. The Jewish leaders wanted to kill Jesus because He made Himself the Son of God.
3. Pilate knew Jesus was innocent and now feared He was the Son of God.
4. A. Pilate is taking Jesus back to question Him to see if He can determine if Jesus is deity or not. B. Jesus is keeping silent.
5. Pilate is boasting of his power over Jesus.
6. A. Pilate's power was given to him from above. B. The Jewish leaders had the greater sin.

Outline:
- The chief priests and Jewish leaders have been trying to trap Jesus and have plotted His death for a while now.
- Jesus's sin is calling Himself the Son of God. This wasn't a sin because He was the Son of God.
- The Jews considered this blasphemy.
- Pilate wanted to appease the crowd, but he didn't want to be responsible for the decision to kill Jesus.
- Pilate thinks Jesus may be deity.
- Jesus fulfills prophecy by keeping silent before His accusers.
- Pilate boasts.

- Jesus lets him know that he could have absolutely no power over Him unless the Father, God allowed him to have it.
- The greater sin is on the false accusers who took Him to Pilate.

Thoughts to Ponder:

1. Are you a people pleaser?

2. Tell me what the writer of Galatians says about those who pervert truth to please people? Galatians 1:10

3. When Peter and John were told they could not speak in the name of Jesus, how did they respond? Acts 5:29

Challenge: Decisions are difficult to make when emotions are heightened. Make decisions based upon facts as much as possible.
Make a solid decision to do what you need to do to care for yourself and stand your ground with any bully.

Write a prayer and ask the Lord to help you to choose your battles carefully and to have the strength to be courageous to make the right decisions for your life.

Book of John

Day 92

Jesus the Spotless Passover Lamb.

*But they cried out, "Away with Him, away with Him!
Crucify Him!" John 19:15*

1. A. Where is Pilate's heart now?

   B. What game are the Jews playing?

John 19:12 NKJV
From then on Pilate sought to release Him, but the Jews cried out, saying, "If you let this Man go, you are not Caesar's friend. Whoever makes himself a king speaks against Caesar."

2. Where is Pilate's heart now?

John 19:13 NKJV
When Pilate therefore heard that saying, he brought Jesus out and sat down in the judgment seat in a place that is called The Pavement, but in Hebrew, Gabbatha.

3. Contrast this verse with John 19:5. Where is Pilate's heart now?

John 19:14 NKJV
Now it was the Preparation Day of the Passover, and about the sixth hour. And he said to the Jews, "Behold your King!"

4. Where is the heart of the crowd?

John 19:15 NKJV
But they cried out, "Away with Him, away with Him! Crucify Him!" Pilate said to them, "Shall I crucify your King?" The chief priests answered, "We have no king but Caesar!"

5. What's happening now?

John 19:16 NKJV
Then he delivered Him to them to be crucified. So, they took Jesus and led Him away.

6. A. Where did they take Jesus?

John 19:17 NKJV
And He, bearing His cross, went out to a place called the Place of a Skull, which is called in Hebrew, Golgotha,

7. What did they do to Him on Golgotha? (Prophecy Isaiah 53:12)

*Fulfilled prophecy Isaiah 53:12
John 19:18 NKJV
where they crucified Him, and two others with Him, one on either side, and Jesus in the center.

Answers:
1. A. Pilate is seeking to release Jesus. B. Their tactic is manipulation to accuse Pilate of high treason against Caesar.
2. Pilate is still attempting to release Jesus.
3. Pilate went from "Behold the Man" to "Behold your King".
4. The crowd have a heart of murder. They are choosing evil over good and damnation instead of eternal life.
5. Pilate is giving in to the demands of the people to keep the peace and prevent him from being accused of treason.
6. They took Jesus to the Place of the Skull called Golgotha to crucify Him.
7. They crucified Him between two thieves.

Outline:
- Pilate can't find a way to release Jesus without being accused of treason.
- Pilate still wants to release Jesus.
- Pilate sees Jesus as the King of the Jews.
- The Jews didn't realize they were crucifying their own Messiah.
- The Jews had a heart of murder and crying to demand death. They did not know that they couldn't kill Jesus, who is the resurrection life.
- Golgotha is where they crucified criminals.
- Jesus hung between two thieves.

Thoughts to Ponder:
1. Do you speak death or condemnation over yourself or those around you?

2. Can you recognize when your peace is gone?

3. What would it look like to sit and read the Word until peace comes?

Challenge: What would it feel like to actively experience a victorious life? This must be lived internally before it externalizes and becomes reality. Think about all your problems for ten minutes and then move them out of the way and let the rest of your thoughts today be peace.

Write a prayer and ask the Lord to give you insight into your passive thinking that is condemning.

Day 93

Prophecy Fulfilled

And for My clothing they cast lots. John 19:24

1. Did Pilate know who Jesus was?

John 19:19 NKJV
Now Pilate wrote a title and put it on the cross. And the writing was: JESUS OF NAZARETH, THE KING OF THE JEWS.

2. What was the purpose of the sign above the cross?

John 19:20 NKJV
Then many of the Jews read this title, for the place where Jesus was crucified was near the city; and it was written in Hebrew, Greek, and Latin.

3. What was the chief priest's response to Pilate's sign?

John 19:21 NKJV
Therefore, the chief priests of the Jews said to Pilate, "Do not write, 'The King of the Jews,' but, 'He said, "I am the King of the Jews."'"

4. A. Would Pilate bend on what he had written?

   B. Why not?

John 19:22 NKJV
Pilate answered, "What I have written, I have written."

5. What did the soldiers take?

John 19:23 NKJV
Then the soldiers, when they had crucified Jesus, took His garments, and made four parts, to each soldier a part, and also the tunic. Now the tunic was without seam, woven from the top in one piece.

6. What prophecy was fulfilled in this verse?

* Psalm 22:18 This fulfills prophecy.
John 19:24 NKJV
They said therefore among themselves, "Let us not tear it, but cast lots for it, whose it shall be," that the Scripture might be fulfilled which says: "They divided My garments among them, And for My clothing they cast lots." Therefore, the soldiers did these things.

Answers:
1. According to what Pilate wrote "Jesus of Nazareth the King of the Jews", he did know who Jesus was.
2. The sign on the cross told the person's name and his crime.
3. The chief priest didn't like the sign.
4. A. No, Pilate wouldn't bend what he wrote. B. Pilate thought Jesus was innocent and that He really was the King of the Jews.
5. The soldiers took Jesus's garments.
6. The soldiers cast lots for His garment.

Outline:
- God revealed the truth to Pilate.
- Pilate did not have the backbone to do the right thing.
- Pilate wanted to please the crowd.
- But Pilate won when he insisted on writing the sign that said Jesus was the King of the Jews.
- Pilate knew Jesus was innocent.
- It was prophesied that the soldiers were cast lots for Jesus's garment.

Thoughts to Ponder:
1. Can you easily recognize when things are out of balance?

2. What do you do when circumstances are sorrowful and not resolving?

3. What would it look like to take your pain and leave it at the cross and just trust God?

Challenge: I cannot achieve my own peace. I just must repent my way out of anxiety. I do this by understanding that anything heavy isn't mine. Matthew 11:28-30

Write a prayer and ask God to reveal to you any lies that you believe.

Book of John

Day 94

Jesus fulfilled Scripture.

He said, "It is finished!" John 19:30

1. Who was at the cross?

John 19:25 NKJV
Now there stood by the cross of Jesus His mother, Mary, and His mother's sister, Mary the wife of Clopas, and Mary Magdalene.

2. Who was the disciple that Jesus loved?

John 19:26 NKJV
When Jesus therefore saw His mother, and the disciple whom He loved standing by, He said to His mother, "Woman, behold your son!"

3. Why would Jesus turn his mother over to John's care?

John 19:27 NKJV
Then He said to the disciple, "Behold your mother!" And from that hour that disciple took her to his own home.

4. Why is this verse important?

*Psalm 69:21...in my thirst they gave me vinegar to drink.
John 19:28 NKJV
After this, Jesus, knowing that all things were now accomplished, that the Scripture might be fulfilled, said, "I thirst!"

5. What was the purpose of this vinegar?

John 19:29 NKJV
Now a vessel full of sour wine was sitting there; and they filled a sponge with sour wine, put it on hyssop, and put it to His mouth.

6. What was finished?

John 19:30 NKJV
So, when Jesus had received the sour wine, He said, "It is finished!" And bowing His head, He gave up His spirit.

Answers:
1. The women who were part of Jesus's life were at the cross.
2. John was the disciple chosen to take care of Mary, the mother of Jesus.
3. His earthly father, Joseph, was dead, and His brothers did not believe He was the Messiah yet. So, He trusted John to care for her. As the eldest son this was His responsibility.
4. This is another prophecy.
5. It was fermented wine and would intoxicate the person and reduce His pain. Jesus refused it, so He would feel the full brunt of the pain and pay the full cost of sin.
6. Fulfilled prophecy of all Scriptures of the sufferings of Christ. (Ps. 22:18; Isa. 53:3-12)
   - Satan defeated. (Jn. 12:31-32)
   - Salvation is for all. The Jews and Gentiles. (Rom. 10:11-21)
   - Death has no dominion over us. (Rom 5:12-21; 6:9; 8:2)
   - Sin has no power over us. (Romans 6:1-23)
   - Peace between God and man. (Rom. 5:1-11)
   - Freedom from sin and death. (Rom.8:18-24; 14;7-9)
   - Justified by grace through Jesus Christ. (Rom. 3:21-26)
   - Conversion and healing. (Jn. 12:40)
   - A way for man to receive the Holy Spirit. (Jn. 7:37-39; Jn. 14:15-17,23)

Outline:
- The women were sorrowing at the cross for Jesus.
- The Lord sends surrogate parents, children, and others in our lives to love and care for us like family.
- Jesus fulfilled all prophecy written for the coming Messiah.
- Can you receive suffering and identify with Christ? Philippians 3:10
- Death, hell, grave, as well as Satan are defeated.
- The penalty for sin is paid for.
- There is reconciliation between God and man.
- Everlasting life is the promise.
- We are justified by grace through faith.
- Healing is my birthright.
- The Holy Spirit lives in me and makes me one with God.

Thoughts to Ponder:
1. Do you think Jesus's Mother understood that He was the Passover Lamb?

2. When your children are greatly suffering in life, do you feel like you have failed or should have done something different? Can you let them grow and learn through pain?

3. Can you trust God to redeem even our foolish or destructive choices?

Challenge: The command is to humble ourselves that He would lift us up. 1 Peter 5:5-6. Today, practice humbling yourself when you are praised or when you are slandered with criticism.

Write a prayer and ask the Lord to teach you how to humble yourself that you would be kept from the vile monster of pride that would make you exalt yourself and drop you into bitterness or self-pity from too much self-absorption.

Angie Meadows

Day 95

Crucified with Christ

> Our old man is crucified with Him, that the body of sin might be destroyed, that henceforth we should not serve sin. Romans 6:6

1. Why did the Jews want to hasten the death of the men on the crosses?

John 19:31 NKJV
Therefore, because it was the Preparation Day, that the bodies should not remain on the cross on the Sabbath (for that Sabbath was a high day), the Jews asked Pilate that their legs might be broken, and that they might be taken away.

2. What did the soldiers do?

John 19:32 NKJV
Then the soldiers came and broke the legs of the first and of the other who was crucified with Him.

3. Why were Jesus bones not broken?

*Prophecy Ps. 34:20
John 19:33 NKJV
But when they came to Jesus and saw that He was already dead, they did not break His legs.

4. Why would the soldier pierce his side?

Prophecy Zech. 12:10
John 19:34 NKJV
But one of the soldiers pierced His side with a spear, and immediately blood and water came out.

5. What was the purpose of the fulfillment of prophecy?

John 19:35 NKJV
And he who has seen has testified, and his testimony is true; and he knows that he is telling the truth, so that you may believe.

6. Was it significant for His bones to not be broken?

John 19:36 NKJV
For these things were done that the Scripture should be fulfilled, "Not one of His bones shall be broken."

7. What does this scripture testify?

John 19:37 NKJV
And again, another Scripture says, "They shall look on Him whom they pierced."

8. Who asked for His body?

John 19:38 NKJV
After this, Joseph of Arimathea, being a disciple of Jesus, but secretly, for fear of the Jews, asked Pilate that he might take away the body of Jesus; and Pilate gave him permission. So, he came and took the body of Jesus.

9. Was Nicodemus ashamed of Him now?

Why would they bury Him with a 100 pounds of spices?

John 19:39 NKJV
And Nicodemus, who at first came to Jesus by night, also came, bringing a mixture of myrrh and aloes, about a hundred pounds.

10. Some say Jesus wasn't dead, but according to this verse was He dead?

John 19:40 NKJV

Then they took the body of Jesus and bound it in strips of linen with the spices, as the custom of the Jews is to bury.

11. Where did they lay Jesus's body?

John 19:41 NKJV
Now in the place where He was crucified there was a garden, and in the garden a new tomb in which no one had yet been laid.

12. A. Why did they place Him in this tomb?

John 19:42 NKJV
So, there they laid Jesus, because of the Jews' Preparation Day, for the tomb was nearby.

Answers:
1. The Jews wanted the ones near Jesus on the cross dead because the next day was a "high day" or a special holiday.
2. The soldiers broke the legs of the other two on the crosses.
3. Jesus's bones were not broken because He was already dead. This was also prophecy.
4. The soldiers pierced His side to make sure He was dead.
5. The purpose for prophecy is for us to believe the testimony (the prophecies).
6. Yes, if one of Jesus's bones had been broken; He would not have been the prophesied/promised Messiah.
7. This verse is confirmation and fulfillment of prophecy Zech. 12:10.
8. Joseph of Arimathea asked for Jesus's body.
9. A. No, Nicodemus was not ashamed of Jesus now. B. The 100 pounds of spices was fulfillment of prophecy that He would be buried with the rich
10. Yes, Jesus's body was dead.
11. They laid Jesus's body in a garden in a new sepulcher (grave).
12. A. The verse says they laid Him in this gravesite because it was nearby.

Outline:
- Jesus trusted the Father with His physical suffering and death and promise of a resurrection.
- The others on the cross had their legs broken, Jesus did not. This fulfilled prophecy.
- Jesus side was pierced to make sure He was dead. This caused the blood and the water to flow. This proved death.
- Jesus fulfilled all prophecies concerning the Messiah.

- Prophecy was to strengthen our belief.
- Joseph of Arimathea buried Jesus like a king.
- Nicodemus was no longer ashamed of Jesus.
- Jesus was physically dead.
- He would be resurrected from the dead in three days. This Jesus foretold.
- The Chief Priest and Pharisees asked Pilate for soldiers to guard the tomb. (Matthew 27:62-66)

Thoughts to Ponder:

1. Sometimes the plan of God looks devastating before He breathes life on it. What in your life looks dead and needs laid in a grave to stay or to be resurrected only by God?

2. What would be exceedingly and abundantly above all you could hope or think?

3. Write out your future dream and dare to dream it? What has God put in your heart to do?

Challenge: Write out poor behaviors, habits or speech that will block you from your destiny. What would it look like to stop rehearsing past wounds and trauma and rehearse a future of the fullness of a resurrected life?

Write a prayer and ask God for a vision of resurrection of something that is dead in your life.

John 20

Arising Early to Honor Jesus

Mary Magdalene went to the tomb early, while it was still dark, John 20:1

Day 96

1. A. Who went to the tomb?

   B. When?

   C. What did she see?

John 20:1 NKJV
Now on the first day of the week Mary Magdalene went to the tomb early, while it was still dark, and saw that the stone had been taken away from the tomb.

2. A. Who did Mary run to tell?

   B. What did she tell them?

John 20:2 NKJV

Then she ran and came to Simon Peter, and to the other disciple, whom Jesus loved, and said to them, "They have taken away the Lord out of the tomb, and we do not know where they have laid Him."

3. What did Peter and the disciples do?

John 20:3 NKJV
Peter therefore went out, and the other disciple, and were going to the tomb.

4. Did they go slowly or quickly?

John 20:4 NKJV
So, they both ran together, and the other disciple outran Peter and came to the tomb first.

5. A. What did the other disciple (probably John) find?

   B. Did he go in the tomb?

John 20:5 NKJV
And he, stooping down and looking in, saw the linen cloths lying there; yet he did not go in.

6. What did Simon Peter do when he got there?

John 20:6 NKJV
Then Simon Peter came, following him, and went into the tomb; and he saw the linen cloths lying there,

7. What position was the handkerchief in (the one that had been around Jesus's head)?

John 20:7 NKJV
and the handkerchief that had been around His head, not lying with the linen cloths, but folded together in a place by itself.

8. Then who else also went into the tomb?

John 20:8 NKJV
Then the other disciple, who came to the tomb first, went in also; and he saw and believed.

9. Did they know the Scripture that Jesus would raise from the dead?

John 20:9 NKJV
For as yet they did not know the Scripture, that He must rise again from the dead.

10. What did the disciples do?

John 20:10 NKJV
Then the disciples went away again to their own homes.

Answers:
1. A. Mary Magdalene went to the tomb. B. She went early, while it was still dark. C. Mary saw that the stone had been taken away from the tomb.
2. A. Mary ran to tell Simon Peter and the other disciples. B. They have taken away the Lord from the tomb, and we do not know where they have laid Him.
3. Peter and the disciples went to the tomb.
4. They went quickly; they ran.
5. A. The disciple saw the linen clothes there. (The ones they had wrapped Jesus in.) B. No, he did not go into the tomb.
6. Peter went into the tomb.
7. The handkerchief was folded together and placed by itself.
8. The other disciple went into the tomb. (This was probably John.)
9. No, they didn't understand and did not know the Scripture.
10. The disciples went away to their homes.

Outline:
- Mary goes to the tomb early. Maybe she went to grieve. Maybe she went to honor Him.
- Mary wouldn't know that the angel rolled away the stone. (Matthew 28:2)
- Mary's first thought was to tell the disciples.
- Mary did not go into the tomb.
- The disciples ran to the place where Jesus was buried.
- Peter was bold enough to go into the tomb.
- The disciples still don't understand what is happening.
- It is almost time for them to have wisdom and revelation knowledge greater than their fears.

Thoughts to Ponder:
1. Have you ever had a season of exercising the consistent discipline of prayer and Bible reading?

2. What would it look like to set an intention for daily spiritual growth?

3. What do you do when you don't understand the plan of God for your life? Do you shrink back and hide from Him or dig your heels in and pursue God more?

Challenge: Go to bed earlier and arise 30-60 minutes earlier tomorrow to find the presence of the Holy Spirit before you start your day.

Write a prayer and ask the Lord to consistently turn your heart towards Him and to give you the spirit of wisdom and revelation in the knowledge of Him. Ephesians 1:17

Day 97

Jesus calls us by name.

Jesus said to her, "Mary! John 20:16

1. A. What was Mary doing?

   B. Then what did she do?

John 20:11 NKJV
But Mary stood outside by the tomb weeping, and as she wept she stooped down and looked into the tomb.

2. What did she see?

John 20:12 NKJV
And she saw two angels in white sitting, one at the head and the other at the feet, where the body of Jesus had lain.

3. A. What did they say to her?

   B. What did Mary say?

John 20:13 NKJV
Then they said to her, "Woman, why are you weeping?" She said to them, "Because they have taken away my Lord, and I do not know where they have laid Him."

4. A. Who was standing near her?

   B. Did Mary recognize him?

John 20:14 NKJV
Now when she had said this, she turned around and saw Jesus standing there, and did not know that it was Jesus.

5. A. What was the first question Jesus asked her?

   B. What was the second question?

   C. Who did Mary think Jesus was?

   D. What did Mary say to Jesus (who she thought was the gardener)?

John 20:15 NKJV
Jesus said to her, "Woman, why are you weeping? Whom are you seeking?" She, supposing Him to be the gardener, said to Him, "Sir, if You have carried Him away, tell me where You have laid Him, and I will take Him away."

6. A. Then what did Jesus say?

   B. What did Mary say?

   C. What does Rabboni mean?

John 20:16 NKJV
Jesus said to her, "Mary!" She turned and said to Him, "Rabboni!" (which is to say, Teacher).

7. A. What negative command did Jesus give her and why?

Book of John

B. What did He instruct her to do?

John 20:17 NKJV
Jesus said to her, "Do not cling to Me, for I have not yet ascended to My Father; but go to My brethren and say to them, 'I am ascending to My Father and your Father, and to My God and your God.'"

8. Did Mary do what Jesus told her to do?

John 20:18 NKJV
Mary Magdalene came and told the disciples that she had seen the Lord, and that He had spoken these things to her.

Answers:

1. A. Mary was standing outside the tomb weeping. B. Mary stooped down and looked in the tomb.

2. Mary saw two angels in white sitting one at the head and the other at the feet of where Jesus had laid.

3. A. The angels asked Mary, woman why are you weeping? B. Mary answers and explains she is crying because someone took Jesus's body, and she doesn't know where He has been laid.

4. A. Jesus was standing by her. B. Mary did not recognize Jesus.

5. A. Jesus asked Mary why she was crying. B. Jesus asked who are you looking for? C. She thought He was the gardener. D. Sir, if you have carried Him away, tell me where you have laid Him, and I will take Him away."

6. A. Jesus called her by her name, "Mary!" B. Mary called Jesus "Rabboni". C. Rabboni means Master or teacher.

7. A. Do not cling (touch) to me. Because I have not ascended to My Father. B. Go to my brethren and say to them, I am ascending to My Father and your Father, and to My God and to your God.

8. Yes, she went and told the disciples that she had seen Jesus and He had spoken to her.

Outline:

- Mary <u>came early</u>. Mary told the others. Mary lingered where she had last seen Him.
- Mary <u>didn't leave</u> when the disciples went home.
- According to Mark 16 Mary had brought sweet <u>spices to anoint</u> Jesus. But she had <u>no clue</u> how she would get the stone rolled away.
- Mary saw angels and may <u>not have recognized</u> them.
- At first, Mary <u>didn't recognize</u> Jesus. Maybe this was because of her tears.

- Mary only <u>recognized</u> Jesus when He called her by her name.
- <u>Jesus opened her eyes and revealed</u> His resurrected self to a woman first.
- Mary went and <u>testified</u> to others.

Thoughts to Ponder:

1. Do you know how to recall the last thing Jesus said to you when things feel powerless?

2. Move any confusion by remembering an answered prayer or a promise from God.

3. Do you sometimes feel like a second-class citizen that isn't chosen first? *Women in those days would never be qualified to be an eyewitness to an event. Their account or testimony would not matter.

Challenge: Find a co-worker, neighbor, church guest, shut-in, that might not feel included and do something to show them that they are valuable. This could be as simple as a welcoming smile and an introduction or a handshake.

Book of John

Write a prayer and ask Jesus to let you hear Him call your name.

Angie Meadows

Day. 98

Evidence of His Presence is peace.

He (Jesus) breathed on them and said ... "Receive the Holy Spirit. John 20:22

1. A. What day was it and what time?

   B. Why were the disciples behind a shut door?

   C. Who appeared amid them?

   D. What did he say?

John 20:19 NKJV
Then, the same day at evening, being the first day of the week, when the doors were shut where the disciples were assembled, for fear of the Jews, Jesus came and stood in the midst, and said to them, "Peace be with you."

2. A. What did He show them?

   B. Were the disciples glad to see Him?

John 20:20 NKJV
When He had said this, He showed them His hands and His side. Then the disciples were glad when they saw the Lord.

3. A. What did Jesus say again to them?

Book of John

B. What did Jesus tell them He was going to do?

John 20:21 NKJV
So, Jesus said to them again, "Peace to you! As the Father has sent Me, I also send you."

4. A. What did Jesus do after He said he would send them?

B. Then what did He say?

John 20:22 NKJV
And when He had said this, He breathed on them, and said to them, "Receive the Holy Spirit.

5. What did Jesus give them authority to do?

John 20:23 NKJV
If you forgive the sins of any, they are forgiven them; if you retain the sins of any, they are retained."

6. Which disciple was not with them?

John 20:24 NKJV
Now Thomas, called the Twin, one of the twelve, was not with them when Jesus came.

7. A. What did the disciples say to Thomas?

B. Did Thomas believe them?

John 20:25 NKJV
The other disciples therefore said to him, "We have seen the Lord." So, he said to them, "Unless I see in His hands the print of the nails and put my finger into the print of the nails, and put my hand into His side, I will not believe."

8. A. How much time passed before Jesus appeared to them again?

B. What did He say to them?

John 20:26 NKJV
And after eight days His disciples were again inside, and Thomas with them. Jesus came, the doors being shut, and stood in the midst, and said, "Peace to you!"

9. A. Did Jesus know what Thomas had said about needing to put his finger in the nail prints of His hand and His hand in His side?

   B. What was Jesus' purpose in telling Thomas to reach his finger here ... and to reach his hand here...?

John 20:27 NKJV
Then He said to Thomas, "Reach your finger here, and look at My hands; and reach your hand here and put it into My side. Do not be unbelieving but believing."

10. A. Did Thomas acknowledge Jesus?

    B. What did Thomas call Jesus?

John 20:28 NKJV
And Thomas answered and said to Him, "My Lord and my God!"

11. Thomas believed because he saw Jesus, but who does Jesus say are Blessed?

John 20:29 NKJV
Jesus said to him, "Thomas, because you have seen Me, you have believed. Blessed are those who have not seen and yet have believed."

12. Did Jesus do signs in front of the disciples that we do not know about?

John 20:30 NKJV

Book of John

And truly Jesus did many other signs in the presence of His disciples, which are not written in this book.

13. A. Why are these things written?

    B. If we believe, what do we have?

John 20:31 NKJV
but these are written that you may believe that Jesus is the Christ, the Son of God, and that believing you may have life in His name.

Answers:
1. A. It was the first day of the week in the evening. B. The disciples were behind closed doors because they were afraid of the Jews. C. Jesus appeared in the room behind closed doors. D. Jesus spoke words to calm them, He said, "Peace be unto you."
2. A. Jesus showed them His hands and side. B. Yes, they were happy when they saw Him.
3. A. Again, Jesus speaks peace unto them. B. Jesus says, as the Father has sent Me, I also send you.
4. A. Jesus breathed on them. B. Jesus commanded them to receive the Holy Ghost.
5. Jesus gives us the authority to forgive sins or retain the sins of others.
6. Thomas was not with them.
7. A. We have seen the Lord. B. No, Thomas would not believe without seeing.
8. A. Eight days passed before Jesus appeared to them again. B. Again, they were behind closed doors and again He spoke peace to them.
9. A. Yes, Jesus knew Thomas's doubts. B. So Thomas would no longer be faithless, but that he would believe.
10. A. Yes, Thomas acknowledged Jesus.
B. Thomas immediately recognized Jesus and called Him my Lord, and my God."
11. Jesus says to Thomas, Blessed are those who have not seen and still believe.
12. Blessed are those who have not seen and yet have believed.
13. A. These words are written so we may believe that Jesus is the Christ, the Son of God. B. We have life in His name.

Outline:
- Here is God's Plan:
    - Peace vs.20.
    - More Peace vs.21.
    - Breath of Life with the Holy Spirit living in us vs. 22.
    - Addressing our Unbelief vs. 25.
    - More Peace vs. 26.
    - Battle of Unbelief vs. Believing vs. 27.

- Blessed are you who believe without seeing vs. 29.
- Believing Jesus is the Son of God is Life! vs. 32.

Thoughts to Ponder:

1. Do you know how to stop striving and simply receive?

2. What might happen if I retain the sins others have done to me?

3. Might I feel the heaviness of that sin in my body?

Challenge: Count how many times today you are fearful or stressed about something and shift your thoughts to receiving the peace Jesus offers. *Fear not, for am with you... Isaiah 43:5*

Write a prayer and ask the Lord to give you the grace to forgive others of evil done to you. Now they have lost the power to rob you of peace. This does not mean they have access to you to sin against you again. If you find yourself angry in a situation, you have internalized it and need stronger boundaries.

John 21

Jesus is Abundance

"It is the Lord!" John 21:7

Day 99

1. Where was Jesus when he showed Himself to the disciples?

John 21:1 NKJV
After these things Jesus showed Himself again to the disciples at the Sea of Tiberias, and in this way, He showed Himself:

2. Who were the disciples that were at the Sea?

John 21:2 NKJV
Simon Peter, Thomas called the Twin, Nathanael of Cana in Galilee, the sons of Zebedee, and two others of His disciples were together.

3. A. What did Simon say to them?

   B. What did the disciples say to Simon Peter?

   C. How soon did they go fishing?

D. When was it?

E. Did they catch anything?

John 21:3 NKJV
Simon Peter said to them, "I am going fishing." They said to him, "We are going with you also." They went out and immediately got into the boat, and that night they caught nothing.

4. A. In the morning where was Jesus?

   B. Did the disciples know it was Jesus?

John 21:4 NKJV
But when the morning had now come, Jesus stood on the shore; yet the disciples did not know that it was Jesus.

5. A. What did Jesus ask them?

   B. What did he call them?

   C. What was their answer?

John 21:5 NKJV
Then Jesus said to them, "Children, have you any food?" They answered Him, "No."

6. A. What did Jesus tell them to do?

   B. Did they obey?

   C. What happened?

Book of John

John 21:6 NKJV
And He said to them, "Cast the net on the right side of the boat, and you will find some." So, they cast, and now they were not able to draw it in because of the multitude of fish.

7. A. Who recognized Jesus?

   B. What did Simon Peter do when he recognized Jesus?

John 21:7 NKJV
Therefore, that disciple whom Jesus loved said to Peter, "It is the Lord!" Now when Simon Peter heard that it was the Lord, he put on his outer garment (for he had removed it) and plunged into the sea.

8. A. What did the other disciples do?

   B. What were they dragging?

John 21:8 NKJV
But the other disciples came in the little boat (for they were not far from land, but about two hundred cubits), dragging the net with fish.

9. What did they see when they came to the land?

John 21:9 NKJV
Then, as soon as they had come to land, they saw a fire of coals there, and fish laid on it, and bread.

10. What did Jesus tell them to do?

John 21:10 NKJV
Jesus said to them, "Bring some of the fish which you have just caught."

11. A. How many fish were there?

    B. Did the net brake?

John 21:11 NKJV
Simon Peter went up and dragged the net to land, full of large fish, one hundred and fifty-three; and although there were so many, the net was not broken.

Answers:
1. Jesus was at the Sea of Tiberias when he showed himself to the disciples.
2. The disciples at the Sea were Simon Peter, Thomas, Nathanael, James, John and two others.
3. A. Simon Peter said, I am going fishing. B. The other disciples said we are going with you. C. They went fishing immediately. D. It was night. E. No, they didn't catch anything.
4. A. Jesus was on the shore in the morning. B. No, the disciples didn't know it was Jesus.
5. A. Jesus asked them do you have any food? B. Jesus called them children. C. No, we don't have any food?
6. A. Jesus told them to cast the net on the right side of the boat, and they would find some fish. B. Yes, they obeyed. C. There were so many fish they couldn't draw the net in.
7. A. The disciple whom Jesus loved (John) recognized Jesus. B. Then Peter put on his outer garment and plunged into the sea.
8. A. The other disciples came to Jesus in the little boat. B. The disciples were dragging fish.
9. They saw a fire of coals with fish and bread.
10. Jesus told them to bring some of the fish which they had just caught.
11. A. There was an abundance of fish; there were one hundred fifty-three fish. B. The net did not break.

Outline:
- Peter went back to the familiar which was his fishing.
- Peter's friends followed him fishing.
- We can work in the physical realm all night, but when the Master comes things fall into place.
- Jesus gave instructions for success.
- Peter recognized Jesus from a distance.
- Peter was eager and left it all to get to Jesus.
- There was no trouble added to the extra heavy fish. Their nets did not break.
- Jesus comes with abundance.

Thoughts to Ponder:
1. When there is one area of your life that is unstable, go to the Word to ground you. What is your favorite verse in the Bible?

2. Where was the first place you met Jesus?

3. Do you have those you disciple?

Challenge: Find someone who has a heart to listen and teach them something the Lord taught you. Who would this be?

Write a prayer and ask the Lord to ground you and keep you stable in His Word during times of stress.

Day 100

1. A. What did Jesus say?

   B. Did they have to ask Jesus who he was?

John 21:12 NKJV
Jesus said to them, "Come and eat breakfast." Yet none of the disciples dared ask Him, "Who are You?"-knowing that it was the Lord.

2. What did Jesus give them?

John 21:13 NKJV
Jesus then came and took the bread and gave it to them, and likewise the fish.

3. How many times had Jesus shown himself to them since his resurrection?

John 21:14 NKJV
This is now the third time Jesus showed Himself to His disciples after He was raised from the dead.

4. A. After breakfast what did Jesus ask Simon, Peter?

   B. What did Peter answer?

   C. What did he command Peter to do?

John 21:15 NKJV
So, when they had eaten breakfast, Jesus said to Simon Peter, "Simon, son of Jonah, do you love Me more than these?" He said to Him, "Yes, Lord; You know that I love You." He said to him, "Feed My lambs."

5. A. What did Jesus ask him again?

Book of John

B. What did Peter answer?

C. What did Jesus tell him to do?

John 21:16 NKJV
He said to him again a second time, "Simon, son of Jonah, do you love Me?" He said to Him, "Yes, Lord; You know that I love You." He said to him, "Tend My sheep."

6. A. A third time what did Jesus ask Peter?

   B. What was Peter's response?

   C. What did Peter say to Jesus?

   D. What did Jesus command him to do a third time?

John 21:17 NKJV
He said to him the third time, "Simon, son of Jonah, do you love Me?" Peter was grieved because He said to him the third time, "Do you love Me?" And he said to Him, "Lord, You know all things; You know that I love You." Jesus said to him, "Feed My sheep."

7. What did Jesus tell him would happen to him when he was old?

John 21:18 NKJV
Most assuredly, I say to you, when you were younger, you girded yourself and walked where you wished; but when you are old, you will stretch out your hands, and another will gird you and carry you where you do not wish."

8. A. Why did Jesus speak this to Peter?

   B. But what was Jesus' command to Peter?

John 21:19 NKJV
This He spoke, signifying by what death he would glorify God. And when He had spoken this, He said to him, "Follow Me."

9. A. Who was following them?

   B. How is John described?

John 21:20 NKJV
Then Peter, turning around, saw the disciple whom Jesus loved following, who also had leaned on His breast at the supper, and said, "Lord, who is the one who betrays You?"

10. What does Peter want to know about?

John 21:21 NKJV
Peter, seeing him, said to Jesus, "But Lord, what about this man?"

11. What is Jesus saying to Peter?

John 21:22 NKJV
Jesus said to him, "If I will that he remains till I come, what is that to you? You follow Me."

12. A. What was the rumor that spread about John?

   B. Is that what Jesus really said?

John 21:23 NKJV
Then this saying went out among the brethren that this disciple would not die. Yet Jesus did not say to him that he would not die, but "If I will that he remains till I come, what is that to you?"

13. A. Who wrote these things down for us?

B. Is his testimony true?

John 21:24 NKJV
This is the disciple who testifies of these things and wrote these things; and we know that his testimony is true.

14. Do we have a written record of all the works of Jesus?

John 21:25 NKJV
And there are also many other things that Jesus did, which if they were written one by one, I suppose that even the world itself could not contain the books that would be written. Amen.

Outline:
Vs. 13 Physical provisions.
Vs. 15-17 Life Application: If we love Jesus, we will feed his sheep.
Vs. 19 Martyrdom is glorification to God.
Vs. 22 Mind our own business and follow Jesus.

Answers:

1. A. Jesus said to come and eat. B. No, they knew it was Jesus.
2. Jesus gave them bread and fish.
3. Jesus has shown himself three times.
4. A. Jesus asked Peter, do you love me? B. Peter answered, yes, Lord you know I love you. C. Jesus instructed Peter to feed my lambs.
5. A. Jesus asked Peter, do you love me? B. Yes, Lord, you know I love you? C. Jesus's instructions to Peter was feed my sheep.
6. A. A third time Jesus asked Peter do you love me? B. Peter's response to Jesus was grief. C. Peter answers Jesus and says Lord, you know all things; you know that I love you. D. Jesus commanded Peter to feed my sheep.
7. Another will gird you and carry you where you do not wish.
8. A. Jesus was telling Peter by what death he would glorify God. B. Jesus commanded Peter to follow me.
9. A. Jesus commanded Peter to follow me. B. John is described as the one who had leaned on Jesus at the supper and had asked who was going to betray him.
10. Peter wants to know what will happen to John.
11. Jesus says to Peter I will take care of him ... you follow me.
12. A. The rumor was that John would not die. B. No, that is not what Jesus said, he said if I wanted him to live until he returned... what is that to you.
13. A. John wrote these things for us. B. Yes, his testimony is true.
14. No, we do not.

Outline:
- Jesus provides physical sustenance.
- Our love for Jesus will heal our souls.
- The command is to feed the sheep.
- Persecution and our death can be a means of glorifying God.
- Our instructions are to follow Jesus.
- Mind your own business.
- The words of Jesus are true.
- The book of John testimony is true.
- There is so much more than we could ever know about Jesus.

Thoughts to Ponder:

1. Can you recognize when you are out of balance and struggling under the weight of a failure or disappointment?

2. How long does it take to resolve AN internal conflict? Five minutes, fifteen minutes, an hour or two, a week, a month, a year…. Or decades?

A divided spirit and soul needs to not be indulged. A failure needs to be reshaped into a disappointment. Persecution or betrayal into a life lesson. Offense must never be tolerated but shifted to praise. Anxiety met with trust.

Maturity comes through our struggles or can distract us from our purpose.

3. Is your identity based upon the finished work of Christ and is his peace firmly established as a rock foundation to your life?

Challenge: Today, remind yourself that it is finished! Move anything and everything that is tormenting in your life to the altar and let your life reflect Jesus Christ to glorify God through your suffering that you may know Him more.
Philippians 3:10
Lord, I offer you....

Write a prayer and ask the Lord to help you abide in Heaven. *Philippians 3:20 For our abiding is in Heaven, from whence also we look for the Savior, the Lord Jesus Christ.*

What would it look like to **ABIDE IN HEAVEN?**

… Angie Meadows

Appendix A

The Morning Watch: The Sweet Fragrance of God.

John 20:16 Jesus said to her, "Mary!" She turned and said to Him "Rabboni!" (which is to say, Teacher).

Seeking
1. Mary sought the Lord to give Him her precious anointing oil (morning adoration) *Mark 16:1 And when the Sabbath was past, Mary Magdalene, and Mary the mother of James, and Salome, had bought sweet spices that they might come and anoint him.*
2. Mary would search for Jesus and face great difficulties to find Him. *Mark 16:3 "…who shall roll away the stone from the door of the sepulcher!"*
3. Mary would not rest until she had found the Lord she sought.
4. She separated herself from the world.
5. She nurtured a faith that refused unbelief and held onto wonderful promises.

Results
1. Mary found Him—and stood in His presence.
2. Her pure love was met by the love of Jesus.
3. Now Mary understood.
4. She received revelation from an angel. *Mark 16:6 And he (the angel) said unto them, be not afraid. You seek Jesus of Nazareth, who was crucified. He is risen! He is not here. See the place where they laid Him.*
5. She lingered after the others had left.
6. She did not recognize Him until He called her by her name.
7. Mary received her commission. *Mark 16:7 But go, tell His disciples-and Peter-that He is going before you into Galilee; there you will see Him, as He said to you."*

Application
1. Mary knows there is nothing in this world for her that she wants anymore. *Mark 16:9 "…he appeared first to Mary Magdalene, out of whom He had cast seven devils."* <u>She is done with this world.</u>
2. Mary's great love for the Lord brought her forgiveness of much. *Luke 7:47 "Wherefore I say to you, her sins, which are many, are forgiven, for she loved much. But to whom little is forgiven, the same loves little."*

Disciples
1. The disciples waited until He breathed on them the power of the resurrected life. (Divine Experience)
John 20:22 …He breath on them, and said unto them, Receive the Holy Spirit.
2. Jesus gave them the power to obey His commandments. *John 13:34 A new commandment I give to you, that you love one another; as I have loved you, that you also love one another.*
3. The evidence of true manifestation of the glory of Christ in our hearts is love. *John 13:35 By this will know that you are My disciples, if you have love for one another."*

4. Christ now takes us into His abiding presence and gives them the great commission. *Matthew 28:18-20 And Jesus came and spoke to them, saying, "All authority has been given to Me in heaven and on earth. Go therefore and make disciples of all the nations, baptizing them in the name of the Father and of the Son and of the Holy Spirit, teaching them to observe all things that I have commanded you; and lo, I am with you always, even to the end of the age." Amen.*

<u>**Conclusion**</u>
- Christ's love needs to be met by our love to find its full revelation for others to see.
- True love for Christ sacrifices everything.
- Genuine love won't rest until it is filled with His presence. *Ephesians 5:2 And walk in love, as Christ also has loved us and given Himself for us, an offering, and a sacrifice to God for a sweet-smelling aroma.*
- A walk of love is a sacrifice and an offering of yourself to God and others.

This is the <u>sweet fragrance</u> unto God.

Angie Meadows

Book of John

Angie Meadows

Book of John

Angie Meadows

www.ingramcontent.com/pod-product-compliance
Lightning Source LLC
Chambersburg PA
CBHW050100170426
43198CB00014B/2405